Learn the lessons to break the chains that have you bound and live a life of freedom, peace, and joy. Most importantly, learn that

Love Is Real

Adam Reid

For George, Georgia, and Sarah. Thank you for loving me enough to help me love myself.

Lessons Overview

Author's Note

Part 4: Meet my daughter and my angel, Georgia Reid, who taught me…

Part 5: Appendix

Before we begin this life-changing journey together, there are a few points I need to go over:

1) This is book one of *The Love is Real Series.* In this introductory book, you will be introduced to me and the three most influential people in my development as a man. You will learn of my fall into depression, anxiety, and alcoholism and see the beginning of my rise back to obtaining holistic wellness. My life is different now. I have peace, joy, and love—things I've longed for my whole life and had almost given up on ever obtaining. In book two of the series, *Love Redeems*, we will meet the rest of the people who have helped to mold my life, hear the details of my climb out of depression, and I'll re-introduce myself as the person I am today. In the third and final book, *Love* > ____, you will meet God, yourself, and the rest of the world. I know it feels like some hardcore narcissism to have two books dedicated to me while you, God (He is kind of important, after all), and the whole world are saved for the last book. Well, this series was actually organized, researched, and written as a single book. No one who knows me will be surprised to hear that when I sat down to write my first book, I wrote so much I accidentally made three of them. Since they were written as one gigantic piece, I hope you continue with me through the entire series to hear all that God has given me to say to make a real change in your life.

2) In a book that's mostly about me, what's in it for you? The challenges and lessons presented in this book aren't what somebody thought would sound good. These are all things I have legitimately done, and I can personally attest to the power of every challenge in impacting your life. A lot of the content, especially in Parts 1 and 2, is very heavy. It's stuff that none of us want to talk about, but guess what? They're problems that many of us face. We all wear masks that say we're okay all the time, and it makes us feel as though we are the only people hiding real problems beneath. Today, I'm ripping off the mask and showing the world all of me, the good and the bad. It's my hope that if you've hit a point where there doesn't seem to be a

way out, this will help you realize you are not alone. I was in a very dark place for over a decade. This book is based on the lessons I've learned from people who actually live the kind of life that I, and so many of you, have wanted for so long. It doesn't matter how many times you've messed up; you can make a change. I have a life now I never dreamed possible. That life is waiting for you, and you don't have to struggle for thirteen years like me. I know some of you have been fighting for even longer, and it feels like the battle will never end. The fight is never over until you give up, and you're still here fighting. Commit to making a change, follow along, implement the advice, and enjoy a better life.

3) I know that if you've found your way to this book, you're searching for your path to recovery. It shouldn't be delayed a single second longer. In a world filled with books claiming they have the answers, the last thing you want to do is waste your time. So, how is this self-help book different from all the others? The problem for most of us when working toward any form of self-improvement is that we start out super excited and motivated. We do new things every day and feel great about all of the change we see in our life. Eventually, life returns to some level of normalcy, and other aspects of life begin to divert our attention away from our efforts. The positive momentum begins to slow as the friction of life grinds against it. Since we aren't pushing forward with force anymore, physics says eventually our refinement will slowly come to a halt. Our attention is diverted elsewhere, so we don't even realize that the goals we were recently driven toward are now a thing of the past. This book isn't meant to be just a pleasant read. When I say we're starting a life-changing journey together, that's not hyperbole. The lessons in this series literally rebuilt my life, and they can do the same for you.

I am defined by my grit and perseverance. You're about to read a book that details my self-deprecating past, so please don't interpret that last sentence as boasting or prideful. I only highlight my tenacity to say that I believe I am as mentally tough as anyone I know, and I lost the fight to anxiety and depression for years. I was beaten because mental health issues aren't something that can be overcome through sheer force and determination. I was fighting a fight that could not be won alone by me or you. You can't just willpower your way through cancer. Your work ethic doesn't allow you to overcome a heart attack while it is occurring. You don't refuse to take your insulin for your diabetes because your faith should be enough for you to be healed. Similarly, your willpower and grit won't overcome your mental health struggles. Your mental health problems are not a mark against your reliance on God and belief in His influence over your life. Just because you cannot see anxiety or depression doesn't make their physical, biological causes any less real.

Even if you don't suffer from anxiety or depression, we all go through episodes of mental fatigue. In this book series, you will learn coping mechanisms and lifestyle choices to help you through these times. Every lesson ends with an action challenge that will prompt you to reflect on the lesson in your personal life and will often include an action you'll be challenged to do. That's why I call it an "action challenge." See how creative I am with titles? Feel free to write directly in this book as you've been provided space to do so. It's important for you to physically write your answers because:

- It forces you to slow down. In a world consumed by productivity, many of us rush from one thing to the next, failing to ever actually be present in the moment. In your blur of efficiency and time management, don't be in such a hurry to finish the book and mark it off of your to-do list that you fail to let it actually help. As someone who was the poster-child for obsessively working toward achievement, I've learned firsthand the benefits of writing. The writing process can have an astounding impact on stress and allow for the expression of thoughts that would've never been realized had you not taken the time to unearth them.
- It requires you to make definitive decisions. Instead of having a string of running thoughts, you'll be forced to weigh your beliefs and opinions to choose those that most accurately convey your feelings.

- Writing things down makes them more real. It's not just in your head anymore. You've put it out into the physical world. I find that most of us hold ourselves more accountable when we take this simple step.

Sample Action Challenge

The word love is used 271 times in this book. It's such a commonly used word that we assume there is a mutual understanding of its meaning. Even so, if I asked ten people to define love, it is very unlikely that any two would describe it in the exact same way. We need to be on the same page when talking about love. Without looking ahead to the definition we'll use, define love.

- Love =

The definition I've found to be the most appropriate for love is this: to show someone their beauty, their worth, and their importance. I've spent a lot of my life striving toward this idea of love. Love is more than a feeling. It is a choice. It is the intentional effort to make someone else know they are unique, valued, and treasured. As we discuss love throughout this book, this is the concept I will be referring to.

Still, if you write your response to each action challenge and move on, eventually you'll finish the book and there is no more call to better your life. Without consistent pushing, this book becomes just another temporary surge of momentum. For our time together to have a lasting impact, you have to be able to take away something that extends beyond each action and creates a shift in your mindset. That's why each part will also have a common theme called a *Lifestyle Change* that will connect each lesson. I recommend reading only one or two lessons per day. This pace slows you down so that you can implement the message into your life.

4) I talk extensively about Christ in this series because He is my rock. He is my ultimate reason for everything and is integral to my story. Still, I know you may not believe like me. And guess

what's crazy. It's okay that you don't. I can still love you, and you can still love me. Let's agree to love each other, not in spite of our differences but because of them. The world will be a lot better off when we accept that you don't have to be just like me, and I don't have to be just like you. This book isn't meant only for people who look like me, think like me, or act like me. In fact, I couldn't care less if you are like me at all. I love you. That may feel weird, uncomfortable, or fake coming from someone you've never even met, but it doesn't make it any less true. I love you not because of anything you can ever do. I love you simply because you are a human who deserves love. Christ loved me before I was ever born. What I do with this fact is my choice, and I choose to love. That is the purpose of this book and my life.

5) Each lesson begins with inspiration I received from lyrics, quotes, or bible verses which I pulled from my personal journals. I have suffered from undiagnosed depression since 2004. I began these journals in January of 2014 when I learned of the conception of my daughter. They detail my six-year journey to discovering holistic wellness. What I've pulled from these sources is interwoven with my own thoughts in my journals because I never anticipated sharing them with anyone else (so I wasn't documenting my sources in MLA format in my journal; shame on me). I've tried to cite as accurately as possible, but these lessons are a part of my daily life. The line between the original concept and my interpretation of that idea has become blurred over the years. I present these passages in isolation to convey my interpretation of their meaning and significance to me. To understand the author's original message, please refer to the sources listed at the end of the book.

6) While writing this series, a lot of the demons I thought I had defeated resurfaced. I fought pride pushing me to write what I thought would sell more books. It was such a large, consuming project that my workaholic tendencies and need for accomplishment started hindering my health and relationships. I struggled with the fear that someone out there needs to hear what I'm trying to say and that I wouldn't be enough to help you. I faced guilt in reliving so many things I want to forget. This all

culminated in an escalation of my anxiety, hurting both my mental and physical health. I know myself well enough that I foresaw all of these problems before I ever wrote the first word, and I decided to write anyway. I know not all of you have been blessed[1] like I have with people who have loved and guided you. I wrote this book for you. More than anything in this world, I hope to help you avoid the stumbling blocks that hindered me for over a decade. At the end of the book, I invite you to have me walk beside you on your journey to discover love and joy in your own life. They're already there. You just have to be reminded of where to look. Ultimately, though, it doesn't matter if you walk with me, only that you walk with someone. Do not suffer alone. Don't throw away years of your life like I did. Make a real change. Leave a legacy that will impact not only your life but the lives of generations to come.

7) Even though the stories in my opening lesson will not paint me in the best light, I have to own every despicable act described. They reveal the person I was and hid for so long. This book series is a combination of my confession for all my sins, and my plea for others to not follow in my footsteps. The *Love is Real Series* is derived entirely from my struggles and the lessons I learned trying to pull myself out of them. I fought through darkness for so long. I clung to every lesson I could learn to help me make it through one more day, to not let today be the day I gave up. I fought so hard for a life that was real. This is my love letter to the world, and every single word of it is true.

---

[1] *When I use the term blessed, I do not mean to indicate that God has given me special favor due to any personal achievement. Quite the opposite. I am blessed because He has given me much more than I deserve. This has everything to do with His grace and nothing to do with my doing.*

Part 1: Meet me, the person who taught me...
Lesson 1: failure is real (and I will never be enough).

I, myself, am made entirely of flaws, stitched together with good intentions.

- Augusten Burroughs, author

I know the bottle ain't to blame, and I ain't trying to.
It don't make you do a thing, it just lets you.
- "Women Without Whiskey" by Drive-By Truckers

The opposite of courage is not cowardice; it is conformity.
- Rollo May

I reached the lowest point of my life in November 2017. A lifetime of pride and self-reliance had finally caught up with me. A lot has changed since then, and I no longer believe negative things about myself that are untrue. As hard as it is, we have to start here on the journey through the lessons that guided me from this place. I'm going to let the person I am now step aside so you can meet the person I was then, or at least how I saw myself:

My name is Adam Reid. I have been a success in most everything I have ever attempted. As I sit in my living room alone and in silent darkness, I have been blessed beyond belief. My life is filled with people who love me and push me to succeed, which has allowed me to achieve every major goal I have ever set for my life.

- I am a son to amazing parents.
- I have been the nephew of George West, one of the greatest people to ever walk the Earth.
- I have a wonderful home in Midway, KY. There is absolutely nowhere I would rather live.
- I am a teacher at Madison Central High School. My classroom walls are covered with notes from students telling me how I've impacted their lives. There is literally no more real estate on my walls to display the messages, so I have a drawer full of them as well. I care deeply about my students, and they return my love in

full. I wholeheartedly believe I have been able to positively impact the lives of fifteen hundred kids. Consistently, my classes score among the best in any possible metric. I have had seven different principals and vice principals tell me I am one of the best teachers in the school or one of the best teachers they've worked with.

- I have been a track and football coach. I love both sports personally and have treasured the opportunity to pass my knowledge and love on to others. I have coached a district champion team and Division-I athletes in football. Our track teams are consistently regional champs, and I've trained a state champion triple jumper.
- Almost all of my best friends have been in my life since I was a kid. They are the most dependable, trustworthy group of guys I could ever hope to know. There is not a doubt in my mind that each and every one of them would drop everything in their lives to be there for me without hesitation.
- I have been a husband to a woman who is a good person and a great mother. She is a nurse who works hard and loves her job.
- At the very center of everything, I am the daddy of Georgia Lynn Reid. She is everything I have ever wanted.

This is everything I ever wanted out of life, but as I sit here alone, I see it is all a mirage. It is all a lie. I am empty. No one in the world knows the deepest parts of me. If I were to ever let anyone see past my mask of success, they would know:

- I have suffered deeply from depression for over a decade. There isn't a person alive who knows of my mental health struggles. In July of 2004, I let down my hero in an unforgivable, unfixable way. Since then, my depression has stealthily grown into a blackness that shrouds everything in my life.
- There is nothing that can be done to change my mistake, so I bury it. I live my life trying to cover it up. I am consumed by my drive for perfection as I try to outrun

my past. I work incessantly to prove my worth and compulsively serve others. I am terrified that if I don't, they may see the real me. And no one could love the real me.

- The only time I am not suffocated by my drive to succeed is when I am drunk. I drink to silence my internal shame. It is my only refuge. So, when I drink, it is to embarrassing extremes. It would take an additional book to list all the mistakes I have made, so I'll list a few of the many.
  - As my addiction and tolerance grows, I have to drink more and more to escape reality. For several years in college, I bought a fifth of cheap bourbon for myself four or five nights a week. The other nights I drank in excess of fifteen beers.
    - I once was a participant in a study by the University of Kentucky examining the impact of alcohol on driving ability. I would show up for a session and take a breathalyzer to ensure I hadn't been drinking before. Then, I would be given varying amounts of alcohol, retake the breathalyzer to determine my impairment, and participate in a driving simulator. I had one of these sessions at 6:00 p.m. and failed the breathalyzer before beginning the session. I had not had a drink that day, but I had been so drunk the night before that I still blew a 0.036 over fifteen hours later
  - I drink to such extremes that I lose control of all mental and physical capacity. It is not uncommon for me to pee myself in my sleep. This is incredibly embarrassing to write even years later.
  - Countless times, I have stumbled as an incoherent zombie down sidewalks beside busy streets. It is a miracle I haven't fallen into the

road and been killed. I wake up in random places without knowing how I got there. Several times, the random place was a jail. On one occasion, it is a hospital bed after I have been driven in an ambulance to the hospital because the cops who picked me up outside of the bar feared for my health due to the severity of my intoxication.

○ I will share details of one of my drunken escapades. This is to show how preposterous my life had become, not to make light of the severity of my issues. On one occasion, I spent the day drinking whiskey, sometimes chasing shots with ketchup, mustard, or mayonnaise to be cool (yeah, that sure was cool). That night, we stood around a fire playing "Hot Piece of Coal" where you do exactly what it sounds like: pull out a burning hot piece of coal from under a fire and pass it around from hand to hand. That morning, I woke up at a friend's house at 5 a.m. having peed myself on their couch. Ashamed for the people there to know, I grabbed a pair of sweatpants from their dryer and set off to walk home. It was a five-mile walk beside one of the primary roads in Lexington, KY. I was still drunk from the night before and never bothered putting on shoes or a shirt. About a mile into the trek, I noticed the pants were so big that I had been holding them up around my waist the entire walk. I searched for a string to tighten them but could not find one. I was confused as to why my friends owned such a large pair of pants since both of them were average-sized people. I shrugged it off and kept going. Another half mile or so later, I began to wonder why they had purchased a pair of capri-style sweatpants. Although they were huge around my waist, the legs were short and tight. I once again accepted this irregularity and kept on walking. I was three miles into the walk before I noticed something dragging the ground between my legs. I stopped and looked down. I was thoroughly confused as to why this huge-waisted, tiny-legged pair of pants also had a third leg. It only took me three miles to piece together the mystery that I wasn't wearing pants. I am a real Sherlock Holmes. I was walking beside one of the busiest roads in the second-largest city in Kentucky with no shirt or shoes and wearing a hooded sweatshirt as pants. Cars continually drove by with families on their way to Sunday morning church. I was over halfway home by this point so I have no other option but to continue my walk in shame.

o That is the story as I have told it often. Friends used to bring it up at parties for me to rehash for people new to the group due to its absurdity. What I always left out in my recounting of the events is that the reason I was drinking to such extremes was my constant mental turmoil. I didn't share with people as they laughed heartily that for the next week I couldn't look in a mirror without getting physically ill because I was revolted by who I had become. I was drowning in my sin and too proud to call out for help. My life was a joke that wasn't funny.

o I am perpetually frustrated and angry. I contain these negative emotions while sober. When I drink, it spews out onto everyone I care about and everyone who cares about me. I say horrible things to anyone within hearing distance, demeaning them and pushing them away. I often threaten to fight people even though I struggle just to stand. I pathetically talk about how I'm the strongest man pound for pound and make a complete joke of myself. Every morning I wake up from a night of drinking, the first thing I do is feel my face to see if I've been punched the night before.

- Nine months from now, I will be arrested for a DUI after driving for several hours with no memory of doing so. Unforgivably, this is not the only time I've driven drunk and risked the lives of innocent people. One of these times, I got home from a bar, and my baby Georgia was crying for me. I tried to pick her up, but she slipped from my unsteady arms and stumbled down some steps. I didn't even know this happened until Georgia's mom told me almost a month later.
  - I am an alcoholic in denial.
- I am selfish. I am impatient. I am prideful. I am judgmental. I am unforgiving. I am manic.
- I have spent my life rebelling against fear or any hint of weakness. I am afraid of heights. The first time I was ever on a plane, I jumped out of it with a parachute on my back. I attack all of my fears and doubts head-on in a similar fashion. This bravado is a sham as I am unable to face the ultimate fear that has dictated every decision of my adult life: I am not enough. This small seed of doubt was planted thirteen years ago and has blossomed into an oak of unyielding, undeniable truth.
- I try with every breath to exude strength and bravery, but I am a coward. I desperately cling to conforming my life to what it should be. I refuse the vulnerability required to actually become the person I pretend to be.
- I try with every breath to give love but fail.
- I have been blessed beyond belief to be supported by loving people who have given me every opportunity to succeed in life. I have spit in the face of these blessings and squandered them all. I am unworthy of all that I have been given.
- Simply put, I am pathetic.

So, I sit in my living room in silence and darkness on this November night in 2017. I am alone not only physically but in every sense of the word. I have fought every day of my life to be good. To be better than I am. To make a difference.

Sometimes I succeed. Sometimes I fail. But I am always empty. I am always alone. Even in a room full of people who love me, I am alone. My daughter, Georgia, took at least some of the emptiness away. She gave me a purpose, a reason to be better. I've made some progress. On this night, even though I'll start back drinking next week, I haven't had a drink in fourteen months. Even so, Georgia's mother and I have finally decided to get a divorce after years of a distant, loveless marriage. She is a good person, but we simply never loved each other. We have put off our inevitable separation because neither of us wants to lose Georgia. Tonight, we accepted that we cannot let our facade of a marriage be what Georgia bases her understanding of love on.

I am exactly where I deserve to be. I deserve to be miserable. I deserve to be alone and unloved. I do not deserve forgiveness because I am too much of a coward to even admit I need it. I have failed at the most important thing in my life: protecting and providing for my daughter. I am defined by my failure and the fact that I am not enough. I will never be enough. Georgia is my reason for living, but now I will only have her half the time. She is the reason for everything good in my life. She is my heart. How can a person live without their heart? I am scared.

I have been a man with ambitions of making the world a better place since my earliest memories. I have spent my life working toward this goal with every sober breath. As a child, I tried to make sure the kids who were outcasts felt included and cared for. I give love and respect to everyone I meet. I tried to be a loving, caring husband. I have tried to be the father Georgia deserves. And I have failed. I appear to have been a success in everything I have ever worked toward, yet I am a failure in every imaginable way. Sitting alone in my living room with my life in shambles, I open a book called *The Daily Office* and read the following passage:

When I was young, I set out to change the world. When I grew a little older, I perceived this was too ambitious, so I set out to change my state. This too I realized was too ambitious, so I set out to change my town. When I realized I could not even do this. I tried to change my family. Now as an old man I know that I should have started by changing myself. If I had started with

myself, maybe then I would have succeeded in changing my family, the town, or even the state—and who knows maybe even the world.
- Hassidic Rabbi on his deathbed

As tears roll down my face, all I can wonder is how my life would've been different if I had just started with me. If instead of trying to change the world, I had tried to change myself. If I had been a better man, if I had been more. I would still have my daughter. I would still have my heart. I cry myself to sleep, knowing nothing will ever be good again. I vividly dream about all the harm I've done by being me.

Failure Action Challenge

I'm just going to come in hot with this first action challenge. This book isn't meant to be just a pleasant read. If you close the pages for the last time and haven't made actionable improvements in your life, then our time together has been a waste. When you dip a toe in the water to test the temperature, you can decide to pull your foot back out. Even if you get in the water, it is often a slow, arduous process. If you want your life to be real, you have to be willing to shine a light in the darkest corners. Instead of putting a timid toe in the water, let's just jump right in. Let's go all the way under and make the decision to be completely invested in improving your life.

Lesson 1 details the lowest moment of my life. Everything in me screamed to give up, to never get out of that chair. It was difficult reliving that moment, but I refuse to run from my pain anymore. It is real. If I can't bring myself to examine this moment and what led to it, then I can never move past it.

Even if your struggles were in no way self-induced, ignoring it keeps you hostage to that moment. It is always there, always lurking in the background. For you to accept it and move forward, you have to understand it. I don't want you to feel pain, but to feel happiness you must accept feeling pain as well. Selectively numbing emotions is biologically impossible. As we progress together, we will work to finally move past this moment. For many of you like me, it may be the first time you've truly tried to live since it happened. In order to move forward, let's first look back.

- Describe the lowest moment of your life. Include as many details as possible: what happened, what circumstances led to the moment, what emotions you felt, how you processed the pain, how your processing (or lack thereof) impacted you and the people you love.
  - Note: I understand that if you are currently in this lowest moment, it will be tough to do this. I personally needed something like this to push me to deal with my issues and to stop my avoidance. Still, this book isn't for me, it's for

you. If the time just isn't right for you to process this moment, then use the option below instead.

- If you felt it was best to not do the option above, describe a high point in your life that you'd like to get back to. In your description of this pinnacle moment in your life, include how you were handling negative emotions differently then and what specifically about this moment you would like to reclaim? What did you like about yourself at this time?

Part 2: Meet my uncle and hero, George "Bubby" West, who taught me...

George at Myrtle Beach

George (left), me (middle) and Alan, my brother (right)

George (left) and his brother, Dave (right) as kids

George in one of his many childhood ninja armors

My dad (left) and George (right) at Myrtle Beach

Me (left), George (middle) and Alan, my brother (right), at Myrtle Beach

My mom (left) and George (right) at Myrtle Beach

Lifestyle change[2]: We spend so much time on work, achievement, notoriety, etc. that we lose sight of the things that really matter in our lives. Cherish the people you love. Each and every one of them. While you read Part 2, I want you to be proactive in realigning the priorities in your life by spending time with the people you care about. Instead of working that extra hour at home, take your dog for a walk, build a fort with your kids, go out for coffee with friends. Don't get so caught up in planning for the future that you forget to live today. Life is meant to be lived together. Live it.

Lesson 2: courage is real (and superheroes do exist).

[8] We are pressed on every side by troubles, but we are not crushed. We are perplexed, but not driven to despair. [9] We are hunted down, but never abandoned by God. We get knocked down, but we are not destroyed.

- 2 Corinthians 4:8-9

[31] What, then, shall we say in response to these things? If God is for us, who can be against us? [32] He who did not spare his own Son, but gave him up for us all—how will He not also, along with Him, graciously give us all things? [33] Who will bring any charge against those whom God has chosen? It is God who justifies. [34] Who then is the one who condemns? No one. Christ Jesus who died—more than that, who was raised to life—is at the right hand of God and is also interceding for us. [35] Who shall separate us from the love of Christ? Shall trouble or hardship or

---

[2] *The Lifestyle Change introduced at the start of each part is an umbrella that covers all of the lessons within that part. Instead of looking at each action challenge as a one-time occurrence, the Lifestyle Change reminders at the end of each lesson will connect these lessons so you feel your actions every day building toward an authentic, lasting revolution in your life. Each lesson helps you achieve the Lifestyle Change. Each time you read a lesson, make sure you take it in the context of its connection to the other lessons in that section and the Lifestyle Change. Ultimately, the actions you take while you read are not going to make this book matter in the long term. Instead, the success of our time together will be measured by how it impacts the decisions you make a month, a year, a decade later. A lasting lifestyle change will only happen if you take the things we discuss in this book out into the real world.*

persecution or famine or nakedness or danger or sword? [36] As it is written: "For your sake we face death all day long; we are considered as sheep to be slaughtered." [37] No, in all these things we are more than conquerors through Him who loved us. [38] For I am convinced that neither death nor life, neither angels nor demons, neither the present nor the future, nor any powers, [39] neither height nor depth, nor anything else in all creation, will be able to separate us from the love of God that is in Christ Jesus our Lord.

- Romans 8:31-39

[12] Blessed is the one who perseveres under trial because, having stood the test, that person will receive the crown of life that the Lord has promised to those who love Him.

- James 1:12

Notice that the stiffest tree is the first to crack while the bamboo sways with the wind.

- Bruce Lee

...dance in defiance of the dark.

- Stephen King, 11/22/63

This book, like all good things in my life, has been inspired by George Alan West. He had to live courageously well before most kids have ever heard of the word courage.

I spent every possible moment with George growing up. He was the epitome of all things cool. Everything in my life I did because I thought that's what he would want me to do. While everyone else was talking about *Saved By The Bell* and *The Power Rangers* at school, I scoffed at their childish ways. (Nevermind the fact that I would sneak and watch both shows when I was alone. The White Ranger is the man.) We used to play a game while driving where we would receive one point for naming the band and one for the song title as they came on the radio. I never won a single time. It seemed as though George knew every tune. This wasn't surprising to me since I was confident that he knew everything about everything. It wasn't until years later I realized that when I wouldn't immediately answer, he'd just make up some song and band name. He never let me win in anything, even if it meant bending (i.e. completely breaking) the rules a little. It makes me smile thinking of how he always challenged me, even as a child. He always told my mom that my brother and I were like his sons. He molded me into one of the most competitive people on the planet. He never treated me like a kid; I always felt like his equal.

Today, my daughter sleeps with a fan on because I do. I sleep with a fan because he did. I even wore leather pants once because he did. Forgive me—the late 90s and early 2000s were a strange time for me. I longed to be as brave as him, to look any challenge in the eye and never flinch. He admired Sho Kosugi and Bruce Lee for their strength and viewed them as heroes who were indestructible. That's the way I looked at him. He was my hero. My superhero. I tried to live in such a way that he could experience the things he missed out on in life through me.

Because of this, I chose biology as the subject I would teach largely because I wanted to understand his life. Brace yourself because I'm about to go through a fairly detailed description of George's disorder. It's okay if you don't understand all of it because it's not essential for our purpose. I just wanted to convey the severity of his struggles.

In a typical heart, there are four chambers: two ventricles that pump blood to the body and two atria that receive blood back from the body. Blood flows away from the heart through arteries. The two primary arteries leaving the heart are the pulmonary artery and the aorta. The right atrium receives deoxygenated blood which then flows into the right ventricle, where it is then pumped through the pulmonary artery to the lungs to get oxygen. The oxygenated blood returns to the left atrium where it then flows to the left ventricle to be pumped out of the aorta to the body. The left and right side of the heart are separated by the septum, ensuring that the deoxygenated blood and oxygenated blood never mix. Oxygen is essential because, in addition to food, it is the other ingredient in cellular respiration for making ATP (what your body uses for energy). This is why you breathe heavier in response to exercising.

George was born with a rare heart disease called transposition of the great arteries with a single functioning ventricle. Instead of two ventricles, the right containing blood without oxygen and the left blood with oxygen, he had a singular enlarged ventricle where all oxygenated and deoxygenated blood mixed. His secondary ventricle was diminutive and nonfunctional. Transposition of the great arteries means that instead of the pulmonary artery extending from the right ventricle and aorta from the left, these two arose from the opposite sides (the pulmonary artery from the functioning left ventricle and the aorta from the non-functioning right ventricle). Due to an aortic valve deformity, essentially all blood flowed into his left ventricle with oxygenated and deoxygenated blood constantly being mixed there. A small hole in his septum allowed some blood into the deformed right ventricle, but its lack of contractile force meant that blood was propelled by the singular contraction of the left ventricle. Consequently, instead of having a one-way flow of blood with deoxygenated blood returning to the heart and oxygenated blood leaving the heart to travel back out to the body, the blood his body received was partially already used and thus devoid of oxygen.

Below is a diagram of a heart with normal anatomy contrasted with George's heart. His disorder is rare enough that I cannot find an image of his exact diagnosis so I've included my sketch for comparison.

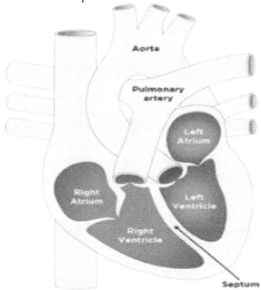

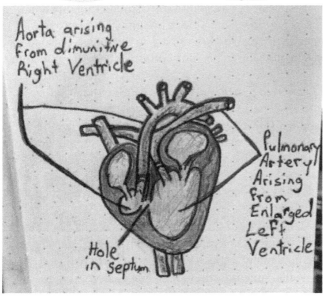

.I've spent most of my life studying the human body trying to understand what he endured. I completed every course in college necessary to enroll in medical school to become a cardiac surgeon. I planned to work exclusively with patients who have his birth defect. I took a break from drinking before my exams to live in the library for a night so my grades would stay at an adequate level. Despite maintaining a 3.9 GPA at the University of Kentucky, I never applied to medical school. I realized that all I had ever really wanted to do was teach. Ultimately, I knew that George would want me to pursue my passion.

In the most basic terms, George is a medical miracle. In all my studies, I have never found how he could have survived for nineteen years before his transplant. I believe with everything in me that his willpower and courage played an immeasurable role in his survival. God had a plan for him, and from the moment of his birth he fought to stay alive to fulfill it.

This heart abnormality accounts for less than one percent of all heart defects. At the time George was born, there was little they could do to treat him, and life expectancy was very short. Over ninety-nine percent of children born with this defect died within their first year. He was constantly smothering due to an inadequate oxygen flow, so his body attempted to improve oxygen intake by increasing blood flow to the lungs. This led to pulmonary hypertension in his lungs, ultimately destroying both organs.

His life was punctuated by one death sentence after another. Doctors proclaimed, rightfully by all medical standards, that he would not live a year. Then, after his first birthday, they moved the life expectancy to five years. Once he turned eleven and was inexplicably still alive, we were told he could not possibly live another year, two at the absolute most. Every year, my family would celebrate George's birthday knowing it could be our last together.

My daughter Georgia turned six years old on September 3, 2020 (I'm writing this passage eleven days later). Her biggest concerns are how many kitties she will get to pet today and her quest to prove that unicorns are real. When George was six, he told his mom he wouldn't mind dying, but he was afraid he wouldn't know anyone in heaven. Around the same age, he told his mom he was worried about what he would wear if he died because he knew they could not afford to buy him a suit.

When he was nine years old, he was especially sick. In a life filled with hospital stays and death knocking on the door, this time period was even worse than most. My mom was pregnant with me, and they wanted to do something special for him. My brother, Alan, was already named after him (George's middle name was Alan) so they decided to let George name me if I was a boy. This seems to be a dangerous tactic, letting a nine-year old name your kid with no limitations. Even so, they were certain I was going to be a girl. (Side note: I know you're wondering, how could they mistake the manliest man to ever be a man for a girl? It's a mystery to me as well.) When I was born and graced the world as a budding beacon of manhood, George proudly pronounced my name to be Sho Kosugi Lee. George could never run or live out any of his fantasies so he idolized martial artists. He derived my name from his icons, Sho Kosugi and Bruce Lee. My parents did not feel that Sho Kosugi personified their chalky white baby. After lots of begging and pleading, they convinced George to let them change my name to Adam. He conceded but under the stipulation that I would know my name, Adam Lee, comes from Bruce Lee, not my dad Timothy Lee. Probably why I'm so tough.

George was not only special to our family, but he impacted everyone he met. Every doctor and nurse who ever cared for George was drawn to this positive little boy with unflinching courage. Even in his youth, he never complained about how ill he was. Every time the doctors would ask how he was doing, he would reply simply, "I'm doing okay." This was such a regular occurrence that any deviation from this positivity was reason for alarm. Once, when he was hospitalized at the age of nine, the doctor asked him how he was doing—to which he replied, "Not so good." The doctor told George's mom that this scared him to death because he knew George had to be really struggling for him to have something even slightly negative to say.

When he was thirteen, he was hospitalized for a blood treatment. For reasons unknown to my family, the cardiologist kept delaying the date of the treatment. As the days in the hospital dragged on, his cardiologist finally spoke to them in tears. Dr. Cottrell had been George's cardiologist from the time he was six months old. She had gone to medical school specializing in pediatric cardiology after the death of her own daughter at the age of six. She had also adopted a child with a heart defect who had died around the age of six. Both of these children had heart conditions similar to George, although not as severe as George's. Her personal experience with this disorder helped her to develop a special bond with George as she cared for him deeply. Through tears, she explained to our family that the procedure was so incredibly painful, and she did not want to put George through the treatment because it wasn't going to matter—he only had a month or so left to live anyway. She did not want him to suffer further, but she underestimated the power of George's will to live. George came through the treatment and continued to defy doctor's terminal prognoses.

My uncle George never knew anything but physical hardship. Still, he never once complained. He never said "Why me?" or "I can't do this anymore." I grew up seeing what real courage is. It isn't boastful or self-promoting. It is silent and unwavering. I've modeled my life and my approach to facing my own obstacles after him. Courage doesn't need to be proclaimed because it is simply understood. He knew, as we all did, that no matter the trials he faced, no matter the doctor's prognosis, or the odds stacked against him, he would press on. When he put his mind to something happening, it happened. He could not be beaten.

Courage Action Challenge

- Who is your hero and why? How did this person's courage stand out to you? How did they refuse to conform to what others thought they should be?

- Just a simple yes or no for this question: Are you living a life they would be proud of (would you tell them everything you do behind closed doors)?
- The opposite of courage is conformity. It is being less than you are so that you don't stand out. It is simply accepting yourself to be what everyone else says you should be. The sad thing is, we are all guilty of doing this. Recall a time when you have conformed to worldly expectations instead of taking the action you knew to be right.

- How would the situation described above (and the resulting events) have happened differently if you would have had the courage to be yourself?

- Maybe you are a student who needs the bravery to avoid the pitfalls that can come with irresponsible partying. Perhaps you have acquaintances who use harsh, sarcastic criticism masked as jokes to belittle others. We all have times in our lives where we can choose to blend in, or we can choose to stand out in order to do what we know is right. Cite specific examples where you can begin to show more courage in your life today.

Lifestyle change:
      Go spend time with someone who you know is living courageously and don't let your time together be focused on their courage. If you know someone battling cancer, going through a divorce, or facing a struggle in life, they are still a human being. They are fighting to not be defined by their situation. Stand beside them in that battle. Allow them to have a break from their fight by going to a game, painting, or just sitting down for coffee and conversation. Help them get to do the activities they enjoy doing but might have had to ignore lately due to their current struggle. Give them a reprieve from having to be courageous and instead simply enjoy life, at least for a moment.

Lesson 3: strength is real (and to not pray for tasks equal to my strength).

7. To keep me from becoming conceited because of these surpassing great revelations, there was given me a thorn in my flesh, a messenger of Satan, to torment me. 8. Three times I pleaded with the Lord to take it away from me. 9. But he said to me, "My grace is sufficient for you, for my power, is made perfect in weakness." Therefore I will boast all the more gladly about my weaknesses, so that Christ's power may rest on me. 10. That is why, for Christ's sake, I delight on weaknesses, in insults, in hardships, in persecutions, in difficulties. For when I am weak, then I am strong.
- *2 Corinthians 12:7-10*

[19] Pray also for me, that whenever I speak, words may be given me so that I will fearlessly make known the mystery of the gospel, [20] for which I am an ambassador in chains. Pray that I may declare it fearlessly, as I should.
- *Ephesians 6:19-20*

Through pressure, stress, and adversity, we are strengthened – in our character, in our faith, and in our ability to get out of bed again and give it one more try.
- *Tony Dungy, the first African-American head coach to win a Super Bowl*

[23] Are they servants of Christ? (I am out of my mind to talk like this.) I am more. I have worked much harder, been in prison more frequently, been flogged more severely, and been exposed to death again and again. [24] Five times I received from the Jews the forty lashes minus one. [25] Three times I was beaten with rods, once I was pelted with stones, three times I was shipwrecked, I spent a night and a day in the open sea, [26] I have been constantly on the move. I have been in danger from rivers, in danger from bandits, in danger from my fellow Jews, in danger from Gentiles; in danger in the city, in danger in the country, in danger at sea; and in danger from false believers. [27] I have labored and toiled and have often gone without sleep; I have known hunger and thirst and have often gone without food; I have been cold and

naked. [28] Besides everything else, I face daily the pressure of my
concern for all the churches. [29] Who is weak, and I do not feel
weak? Who is led into sin, and I do not inwardly burn?
- 2 Corinthians 11:23-33

You may not control all the events that happen to you, but you
can decide to not be reduced by them.
- Maya Angelou

Passing the buck. The last refuge of the cowardly and
blackhearted.
- Ron Swanson

Paul was the greatest missionary the world has ever known. He spread the good word of Christ to gentiles throughout the world who, without Paul, would have never been exposed to Him. He risked his life by preaching the Word where the people had completely opposing beliefs. When Paul said Jesus was God, he angered some of the Jews who had condemned Jesus for blasphemy. He infuriated the sect of the Romans who worshiped the emperor as god. When Paul said Jesus was human, he upset a faction of the Greeks who thought divinity was soiled if it had any contact with humanity. He knew that it was literally impossible for his message to be universally accepted, but he pressed on. He stood firm with resolution in the saving grace of Jesus Christ. His care for the churches he helped build during his travels did not cease as he moved on to next locations for his mission. The letters of instruction and support he wrote for these congregations became thirteen books of the New Testament. His unwavering strength and resolve changed the lives of innumerable people.

Paul's dedication to God's message came at a severe personal cost. In Paul's letter to the church of Corinth, he details all he has suffered through. He went to prison multiple times, was flogged viciously, beaten with rods, received lashes, pelted with stones, shipwrecked, and much more. He is in no way exaggerating when he says he has been exposed to death again and again. Paul wrote his letter to the church in Ephesus during his three-year imprisonment for false accusations. Paul was in chains because of the gospel he preached. Paul did not ask the Ephesians to pray that his chains would be removed, but that he would continue to speak fearlessly for Christ in spite of them. Paul trudged unflinchingly toward his purpose not only because of his personal strength, but also because of his unwavering belief in The One from which his strength arose. Through all of his trials, he knew Christ was with him, never leaving or forsaking him.

I honestly don't know how many times we received the call to come quickly because George was dying. Everyone was always distraught, terrified this would be the last moment we would have the cornerstone of our family with us. Their despair was always warranted. Heart attacks and complete body failures obviously are dangerous, terrifying times. Even so, I never really worried when the calls came. Honestly, not a single time. No matter the situation, I had no doubt he would pull through. George was my hero, so I had an irrational belief in his strength. Still, part of my confidence was justified. George truly did have an inner strength and will to live that cannot be described. I knew if he continued to fight, there was no danger of losing him. He was stronger than anything he would ever go through. Time and time again, he proved me right. When there was no way he could survive, he survived anyway.

George's health continued to deteriorate until it reached depths he had rarely experienced in his life. Dr. Michael Sekela had just performed the first transplant of a heart and both lungs in the state of Kentucky. After meeting with George and running preliminary tests, he told our family it was impossible that his heart and lungs had been keeping him alive this long. Dr. Sekela was yet another in a long line of respected medical professionals to conclude that George's life was a miracle. The first successful surgery on the human heart did not occur until 1944 at Johns Hopkins. Before this, it was considered medically impossible due to the necessity of maintaining blood flow throughout the body while the operation on the heart occurred. George had his transplant on November 23, 1993. Fewer than fifty years after the most advanced minds in medicine thought it was preposterous to even attempt surgery on the heart, George had his heart and lungs removed from his body and replaced by those of a donor who had died less than ten hours before. George was the second person in Kentucky to have this triple transplant. He was only nineteen years old.

I believe God often allows the harshest challenges to come to His most faithful servants. It's seen time and time again in the Bible through Abraham, David, Job, and countless more. Even so, I don't believe it is always just to test the faith of the specific individual. I think God has a chosen few who are meant to show the rest of us what is possible through Him.

Words can be cheap. If Paul had leisurely traveled from city to city being welcomed and praised where he preached the gospel, his words could've been interpreted as self-serving or hollow. The people who came to hear Paul speak for Christ knew that this man was risking his life. They saw him beaten, stoned, and imprisoned. Yet his commitment to his message never wavered. Paul prayed three times for God to remove the thorn from his flesh. He prayed that God would simply take the problem away. God replied that His grace is sufficient and that His strength is made perfect in weakness. Our weakness is a reminder of our need for God. After this, Paul never prayed for God to take away the struggles or to ease his pain. He prayed only for the strength to overcome whatever obstacles may come and thanked God for the weakness that forced him to rely on Him.

Just as Paul showed the world what strength in Christ looks like, George did the same for us. He lived a life that taught us quitting was not an option. He was the epitome of unyielding, unrelenting resilience. He had the strength to take on what the rest of us could not. God chose him to be the source of strength not just for himself, but for us all. The strength I have comes from him. I witnessed George face and overcome more than I could ever bear. I was born with no surpassingly great attributes other than this: no matter how bleak the situation or seemingly insurmountable the obstacle, I have held the resolve to continue to push forward toward the mark. This fortitude I owe to the strength I witnessed in the strongest man I have ever known.

When troubles come my way and I feel like begging God to just take it all away, I think back to a man who never once prayed for tasks equal to his strength. Instead, he prayed for strength equal to his tasks. So I do the same.

Strength Action Challenge

- List some of the problems you are dealing with right now.

- Describe how you can show strength in spite of these. If you don't have strength for your sake, find it for the sake of those who are looking to you to see how to handle tough situations.

George couldn't walk across his yard without stopping to catch his breath. I'm not sure if he could've bench pressed the bar, but he was the strongest man I ever knew. He persevered while most other people, including me, would have crumbled. I have spent my life trying to be strong because of his example, but often I have been weak. Even so, every time I wanted to give up, I would ask myself if he would be proud of me. Knowing what he went through and the person he still managed to be, I've found a way to keep going. All the times in my life when I didn't have the strength within me, I found it in him. In *The Edge*, Charles Morse says, "What one man can do, another can do." I've never faced trials like he had to, but I have endured those I have faced for him. If he can, I can.

George didn't just show me strength. To me, he was strength. Without him, everything I knew then and today about strength would be distorted. It is the same with you. The ones you love need to be able to look at you to see strength. Through you, they can learn how to develop their own fortitude to be able to stand against the trials that are destined to come. If you fail to be this example, society will teach them a completely invalid, shallow imitation of what strength really is. We spend our time lifting weights and running miles at least in part to test our strength. In reality, these things have absolutely nothing to do with strength.

There will come a time in the lives of the ones you hold most dear that they're going to head down dead-end roads. For me, it was alcohol. It may be the same for them, or it may be one of a million other temptations. Whatever it is, the time may come when they are lost. Have you lived the life that shows them the way back? People see you when you don't know they're looking. The trials you face today help them overcome the ones they'll struggle with tomorrow. If you can, they can.

Lifestyle change:

Choose someone and have a real discussion with them about strength. How do you see strength in them? How do you try to show strength for them? The acceptance and examination of weakness is essential to this talk. Everyone feels weak at times. How can we show strength even when we don't feel we have any?

<u>Lesson 4: faith is real (and you are who you are during hard times).</u>

[20] Truly I tell you, if you have faith as small as a mustard seed, you can say to this mountain, 'Move from here to there,' and it will move. Nothing will be impossible for you.

- Matthew 17:20

[5] Now no shrub of the field was yet in the earth, and no plant of the field had yet sprouted, for the Lord God had not sent rain upon the earth, and there was no man to cultivate the ground. [6] But a mist used to rise from the earth and water the whole surface of the ground.

- Genesis 2:5-6

Faith is not waiting for the storm to pass. It's dancing in the rain.

- Vivian Greene

[1] Now faith is confidence in what we hope for and assurance about what we do not see.

- Hebrews 11:1

[27] Jesus replied, "What is impossible with man is possible with God."

- Luke 18:27

   Noah trusted God that a flood was coming that would cover every inch of land. That is a commendable leap of faith in itself, but this is even more astonishing when we consider that it had never rained. Ever. God had previously irrigated the earth from the ground up. Drops of water had never fallen from the sky, yet Noah was building a ship to survive a flood of these never-before-seen drops of water. He didn't even question how he was supposed to round up two of every living animal. Noah spent one-hundred and twenty years building the ark. He was ridiculed year after year when no rain came. Every aspect of his task was impossible. A man and his family cannot build a ship to these proportions. A single person cannot manage the immensity of all of the land animals in the world. If he had relied on his own understanding, he would've given up a thousand times over. Instead, Noah believed in God when there was no earthly explanation as to why he should.

I struggle to relate to Noah. How could he possibly believe so strongly to spend one-hundred and twenty years working toward something that has absolutely no logical explanation? Perhaps my biggest weaknesses in my walk with Christ are my self-reliance and need for explanation. I have spent my professional life engrossed in biology and the value of the scientific method. Our department motto was to "Ignite the passion to ask why and help develop the ability to find the answer." Knowing the end results has never been enough for me because I have a need to understand the steps that led to it. In short, I have a scientific mind. I want to hypothesize and experiment until I feel certain of the results, not just in class but in life. I have confidence in things I can see or prove. As such, faith does not come natural to me. If I were placed in Noah's situation, mankind would be extinct. I doubt I would have been willing to even begin work, let alone spend most of my life on this seemingly unreasonable task.

Noah demonstrated faith in God's message even though he had no logical explanation as to why he should. His faith was greater than his need for understanding. Job demonstrated immense faith in another fashion. He was God's most faithful and holy servant. Satan challenged God saying that Job's faith would fade if he were to lose all the gifts God had given him. God allowed Satan to rob Job of everything he loved. He lost all of his belongings. He lost his family. He lost his health. Still, even though everyone else around him pleaded with him to admit his sin and claim that his punishment was righteous, he stood firm in his faith. No matter how Satan tortured him, Job held to his love for God. Eventually, God rewarded Job's perseverance with gifts beyond those that Satan had robbed him of.

Faith comes from a belief that there is something bigger than ourselves, something beyond our capacity for explanation. As I've already said, George's mere survival was a miracle in itself. There is no medical explanation as to how he lived so long and achieved so much despite his heart condition. Yet, I saw him do it. I know, beyond a shadow of a doubt, there is something more. There is a greater power. When there seems to be no way, He makes the way. George's faith rivaled Noah's and Job's. Like Noah, George believed when there was no reason he should. George never once complained about his struggles or denounced God for allowing such pain in his life. George admired Job. I have a copy of George's essay titled "Why Good People Suffer." George studied the life of Job and why he was allowed to suffer as he did. George's conclusion was the same as mine. Great suffering can lead to an even greater faith and immeasurable treasures in Heaven. Like Job, George's faith in God was greater than any challenge the world could present.

Still, unlike these two biblical men, George's faith was not rewarded with an earthly reward. George held onto his belief in a miracle healing until his last breath. He held onto faith for a healing that never came. This would seem to make his faith a failure. He built his life around a belief that ultimately did not come to fruition. But faith is bigger than a singular situation. Faith penetrates all aspects of our lives. George didn't live in fear or dread. His faith allowed him to live his life to the fullest capacity. He was overflowing with love and joy. And he received his healing. It just didn't come in the manner that we all prayed for. George never ran on this earth, but he runs every day today. His few years on this earth were burdened, but his reward is an eternity in heaven where this is no sickness or pain. There are no tears or worries. George held on to his faith because he knew he was already a winner, in this life or the next.

I never saw George's struggles. I only saw the strength. As I've gotten older, I've realized George wasn't the mythological creature I made him out to be. He was just a man. A man like me, Noah, Job, or any other. He faced the same struggles of fear and doubt that we all do. I wonder how many times he prayed for the healing that never came? As his time was running out, he was presented with the miracle of his transplant. This was finally his chance at a normal life. The life expectancy for the procedure was only five years, but those years would be spent doing all the things he had missed out on in his life. He was going to be able to run, to live life fully with no limitations.

He was going to get to enjoy the things we all take for granted. He was going to be able to walk through the grocery store in comfort. He would make plans and know that he would actually be able to follow through with them.

Yet, in the end, George's transplant was another blow to his morale. It did improve his health and extend his life, but he never got the "normal" he prayed for. He still had unexpected health troubles and hospital stays. He was never healthy enough to attend his college classes on a consistent enough basis to graduate or to pursue his professional passion. He never got to move into his own home or live a day that wasn't centered around his health.

Even after this ultimate disappointment in a life punctuated by one letdown after another, he made a decision that defined all other decisions in his life. He decided to pray not for tasks equal to his strength but for strength equal to his tasks. He decided to maintain his joy in spite of disappointment. God hasn't given us the ability to control our circumstances, He's given us the ability to control ourselves. Faith is living life with hope when there is no reason to have it. It is not waiting for the light to cast away the darkness. It is dancing in defiance of the dark. It is living above your circumstances. George did that better than anyone I ever knew. Hebrews 11:4 says, "By faith Abel brought God a better offering than Cain did. By faith he was commended as righteous, when God spoke well of his offerings. And by faith Abel still speaks, even though he is dead." Abel's faith was greater than his life, and so was George's. His faith lives on after him in all of us who were inspired by it.

In the letters I received that will supply the content for the "George in Their Own Words" sections later on, there were also copies of two essays George wrote entitled "The Intervention of Angels" and "Why Good People Suffer." I treasure those as they gave me insight into who George really was as a man. I respect his strength even more knowing he kept it through periods of weakness and doubt. I used to think he was simply too strong to ever falter. Now, I know that was wrong. In fact, he was so much stronger than that. He had the strength to get back up after he fell down. The rest of this lesson is taken directly from George's words. To my knowledge, George never really talked about this with anyone. Here are pieces from one of my most prized possessions.

Excerpts from "The Intervention of Angels" by George West with my comments in parenthesis:

- I was so naive to how sick I truly was. I was afraid they would find I was in too good of health for the transplant. Later, I found out after the test (to decide if he needed the transplant) that Dr. Sekela had diagnosed me with six months to live.
- So, time went on and I finished high school. During the graduation I became sick and had to leave. I never got to walk in my cap and gown. I didn't get to walk up on stage for my diploma like all of my friends. When that happened, I knew I had to have that transplant, no matter what the odds were against me, even if it meant death.
- For the first time in my life, I had hope of a normal life. Part of me felt like I was giving up on God and not holding to my faith for a miracle healing, and another part of me felt like this transplant was God's way of healing me. Either way, I knew if this surgery didn't go right and I passed away, I knew without any doubt in my mind I was heaven bound.
- When we got to the hospital, they began to put in the deep lines and PICC lines into my neck and arms. I realized I had never really been put through real pain like this before. I prayed to myself, "Lord, if this is what it's going to be like, You have to be with me."
- As they rolled my bed out, I saw my brother Dave and cousin Bill. Tears were rolling down their faces, and I began to cry. Not because I was scared or worried about myself, but I was heartbroken to see them so sad.
- The next memory I have is hearing my dad's voice. He was holding my hand and asking me to squeeze his finger if I could hear him. I was unable to move my fingers or even open my eyes. Then, I remember waking up and having my hair washed. My brother-in-law, Tim, was sitting next to my bed. Tim jokingly told the pretty

nurse washing my hair that she needed to do his next. Tim could always cheer me up.

- *Note: Dad said this in a goofball manner, not in a creepy way that would make the nurse uncomfortable. My dad loves his Girlfriend (what he calls my mom) so much, I'm not sure he even realizes there is another woman on the planet.

- To the best of my memory, I wasn't in any serious pain that I couldn't bear but just the most awful feeling anyone could imagine. I can't really describe how I really did feel. Even now thinking back on it stirs up a lot of bad feelings. I was on life support and had tubes and wires running all over my body. I couldn't roll to either side so I had to lay flat on my back.

- (I have not included them here, but George goes on to list lots of the struggles he endured during the first few days after his surgery: hallucinations, being taken off life support, having to learn to breathe like "normal people did," and many more.)

The next memory is that I was in bed with the nurse over me with a mask on my face pumping oxygen into me. She was yelling code blue, then I blacked out again. When I awoke, I found that I had been put back on life support and had a collapsed lung. I was heartbroken that I had taken such a fall in my progress of getting well. I took it really hard. I gave up hope. It was all just more than I could bear. My spirit had been broken. That night as I lay in bed all alone, I prayed to God that he would let me pass away. I prayed that I had made a horrible mistake and now all I wanted was to die. As tears rolled down my face, I quietly asked God, "Why do I have to go through this?" Then, I heard a voice. It was a man's voice, a very calm, soft voice. It sounded as though the voice was coming from the corner of my bed, just behind my head. The voice answered my question and said, "Because Jesus took the stripes so you could be healed." Now, if I was to hear a voice speaking to me right now, I think I would be totally freaked out, but, for some reason, at that time I wasn't. It just seemed natural to be hearing that voice. I didn't even turn to see where it was coming from. After the voice answered me, I spoke back and said, "But, I'm so lonely and scared by myself." Then, another voice answered and said, "When Jesus was crucified everyone turned their backs on Him, and He had to go through it all alone. But, you have a waiting room full of loved one's supporting you." Like the first voice, it was a very calm, soft speaking man's voice. I could see the faces of my family sitting out in the waiting room with such worried looks. So, then, I said, "Well, if I could just have something to drink, maybe it wouldn't be so bad." Then, the first voice spoke again and said, "When Jesus was on the cross and asked for a drink, he was given vinegar." When the voices told me these things I could almost see Jesus. I could almost feel what He went through. So, then I said to the voices, "I'll do my best to get well." Two days later, the life support came off. Even though I still had a long, tough road ahead of me, I had a much better attitude and a stronger will to get well. It was several weeks later that it occurred to me that those voices I had heard were the voices of angels, sent by God to give me the inspiration I needed to get through that ordeal. Some people may dismiss what I heard as only hallucinations, but I know better. I haven't heard or seen anything of that sort since that night. But when things get hard for me, I think back to that night when God's angels spoke to me.

Faith Action Challenge

- List some things you want in your life, and how long you've had this desire.

- Look back at your list. Is there anything you've been waiting on for a year? Five years? All your life? How does waiting on this change impact your daily life? Have you given up faith, or do you still believe?

- I looked to George for my definition of faith. George saw his example of what faith should be in the life of Job. Has there been anyone in your life who has shown you what faith looks like? How do their actions inform the way you maintain your own hopes?

Lifestyle change:

Do you have enough courage to wake up with hope each morning even if you've done so for days, weeks, months, or even years without whatever you're facing getting better? It's never over until you give up. It's natural to want to just lay down and quit. The problem with that is that when you get up the problem is still there. It's up to you to carry on through the storm.

On our own, our faith will wane. It's inevitable. We are human, and we will fall. Today, you're going to be someone else's courage. Reach out to someone who you know may be going through a hard time. Offer support. Don't just say "If you need me, I'm here." People rarely are willing to show vulnerability and admit they need help. Be proactive. Be the support you know they need.

Faith must be more than belief in certain facts. Faith must go beyond what we believe. It must become a dynamic part of all we do. When you reach out to someone today, talk to them about their situation if that is what feels appropriate, but faith is more than words. You can help someone renew their faith through companionship, activity, or anything that rejuvenates the spirit. All of our problems are unique, but the need for relentless hope for overcoming these issues is universal. The belief that one day we will overcome is not just important, it is essential.

Lesson 5: fear is real (and to never go down looking).

[1] God is our refuge and strength, a very present help in trouble. [2] Therefore we will not fear, though the earth should change, though the mountains shake in the heart of the sea; [3] though its waters roar and foam, though the mountains tremble with its tumult. Selah.

- Psalms 46:1-3

[9] Have I not commanded you? Be strong and courageous. Do not be afraid; do not be discouraged, for the Lord your God will be with you wherever you go.

- Joshua 1:9

I have no idea where I am going. I do not see the road ahead of me. I cannot know for certain where it will end. Nor do I really know myself, and the fact that I think that I am following your will does not mean that I am actually doing so. But I believe that the desire to please you does in fact please you. And I hope I have that desire in all that I am doing. I hope that I will never do anything apart from that desire. And I know that if I do this you will lead me by the right road though I may know nothing about it. Therefore will I trust you always though I may seem to be lost and in the shadow of death. I will not fear, for you are ever with me, and you will never leave me to face my perils alone.

- Thoughts of Solitude by Thomas Merton

"You miss 100% of the shots you don't take. - Wayne Gretzky"
- Michael Scott

Although his health never resembled "normal," George did experience years of improved wellness and longer periods without hospital stays following his transplant. This meant he could come to many more of my sports events. I knew that I had been given a gift of having my uncle and my dad in my life. These were the two greatest men I will ever know. I understood that as early as I have memory. These two men sacrificed much of their lives for me, and as such, I wanted my life to honor them. I had to live my life in a way that made their lives worth it, so I put an unreasonable amount of pressure on myself to be perfect in everything. I knew George was never able to run or play sports. I was his chance to get to experience the things he longed to do.

I vividly remember my first year of fast pitch baseball. George was in the stands which was always a huge deal for me. It came down to the situation that all young athletes dream of. It was the last inning and we were down by one. I'm at the plate with the bases loaded and the count is full. To be honest, I was terrified. I was afraid that I would swing, I would miss, and everyone would see I couldn't do it. So before the pitcher ever went into his windup, my mind was already made up. I would not swing. I would do nothing. I just hoped he would throw a bad pitch or the umpire would have a tight strike zone. I decided to let someone else determine my fate. The pitcher wound up and delivered the pitch. I could tell from the moment it left his hand that it was my perfect pitch, just a little low and outside. I had hit that pitch countless times, but I was frozen in fear. I had predetermined I could not succeed so I should not even try. I just stood there and watched it glide by. I was walking back to the dugout with my head hung low before the umpire ever called the strikeout.

On the ride home, nobody really said much. Finally, George said one seemingly small, passing comment. "I can't believe you didn't swing. I thought you could strike out, but I never thought you would go down looking." It was crushing to disappoint him. It wasn't that I had failed. It was that I had failed to even try. My life was shaped by this. I knew George would have swung. If he had been given the gift that I had to be able to pursue anything I wanted in life, he would always swing.

After that, every fastest race I ever ran and every greatest game I ever played in football, George was in the stands. I was never going to be the most talented at anything, so I resolved to never again fail due to fear or lack of effort. I have given every ounce of myself to anything I have ever attempted. Even at thirty-five years old, if I'm playing a casual game of badminton or kickball, it is a guarantee that I'll spend half of the time on the ground diving and leave with scratches and bruises. I have gone the rest of my life refusing to go down looking. Of all my mistakes, and there have been countless, none of them have been because of a lack of effort or a failure to care.

In her book, *Grit,* Angela Duckworth concludes after her years of research that success is primarily determined by grit. She was hired by the Navy SEALS to help them figure out why so many of their best trainees ended up quitting. None of the test scores or physical tests they relied on were a consistent indicator of who would succeed as a Navy SEAL. Often, the candidates at the top of every measurable piece of data ended up quitting anyway. In response, she developed the following formula:

$$\text{Talent x effort} = \text{skill}$$
$$\text{Skill x effort} = \text{achievement}$$

The SEALSs now use a series of tests designed to determine the grit of their candidates. When it boils down to its simplest state, Angela Duckworth's research showed that success isn't determined by brains, brawn, or status. It is determined by grit. To have an unyielding drive toward a singular goal. In the SEALs and in life, the ability to never quit outweighs all else.

I have never had much talent at anything. Still, I have given every ounce of effort I have to everything I've ever done, and effort is twice as important as talent with regard to achievement. No matter how much I feared something, I never feared it more than going down looking. I know I was given the gift of a healthy body and mind, and I have always tried to appreciate that. I don't know the exact number, but I think I had around six Bs total in my life when I received my Master's degree in education. This may seem blasphemous from a former teacher, but I never cared about grades. Still, even after two straight weeks of being blackout drunk through college and rarely going to class, I'd live in the library before every test. I didn't do this because I cared about the grade. I did it because I cared about never being less than I could be. That's the same reason I once finished a mini-marathon without being able to bend my left leg for the last five miles and still hobbled to the finish line in under two hours. I have never had the regret of walking away from a task knowing I could have done more.

Everything I've earned in life has been through grit and effort, and those traits came solely from George. George gave me the gift of knowing I controlled my own destiny, and the effort I put forth would directly correlate with my success. I am proud of the things I have accomplished and the work it took for me to achieve them. I have refused to give up after I have hit rock bottom multiple times with my life in shambles. Eventually, my decision to finally have the bravery to confront my shame and mental health problems will give me a chance to get my life back. Even then, it was only through effort and the refusal to ever give up that I was able to do so.

I've lived with fear just like anyone else, but I've refused to let it dictate my life. I am afraid of heights. The first time I was on a plane, I was jumping out of it. One of my favorite hobbies is rock climbing, and I have a tinge of fear every time I'm on the wall. The more I am afraid of something, the more I want to do it. The most commonly used phrase in the Bible is "fear not." It is used 366 times. Everything I will ever do comes back to this. Fear not. I cannot keep myself from fear, but I can prevent it from dictating my actions. George didn't make me fearless. He just made me want to be greater than my fears.

Fear Action Challenge

Fear is a normal emotion. It can inspire us, but we cannot let it overwhelm and control us. Fear actually primes you to perform better in that moment than you ever could otherwise. Our body's response to fear is called a fight or flight response. Essentially, your body releases cortisol (commonly called adrenaline). This increases heart rate, promotes sweating, and tightens muscles to prime you to fight or run for your life. The reason many of us get nauseous in response to fear is that our body practically shuts down everything we do not need in that moment to survive. We shunt blood away from our stomachs because it doesn't matter if we're digesting our last meal properly if we could die in the next minute. Instead, all of our blood is pumped to our brains to think more clearly and our muscles to react to the brain's signals more efficiently. Accept fear as a normal, necessary emotion. When you feel fear, instead of trying to avoid it, accept that it is your body's way to help you through this difficult moment.

- In our faith action challenge, you listed some things you are holding out hope for. I want to revisit those items but look at them from a different angle. For each response you had, list them here again with specific, concrete actions you have taken to ensure you achieve them.

- There are some things in life we cannot change and must accept. However, I do not know of a single circumstance that cannot be improved by our mindset and actions. I watched a man who suffered constantly and was given a death sentence from the moment of his birth live a more joyful, love-filled life than anyone I have ever met. Look at the list from above. You say you want it, but what have you done to get it? Is fear of failure holding you back? Could you be doing more? Using the same list, what are some additional steps you could take to increase the likelihood of attaining your desires if you were not concerned with fear of rejection or failure.

Lifestyle change:
The thing about scary stuff is, wait for it, it's scary. Life in isolation can be terrifying. The good news is none of us are truly alone. The fear won't just disappear, but we are stronger together. If you are willing to face a fear with someone by your side, you have taken a major step toward overcoming an obstacle in your life. Today, I'm going to give you some options. The fact that you are willing to face a fear in any fashion is a win, so I want you to be able to do so in whatever way feels most comfortable and safe to you.
-   Detail your fears in an open conversation with someone you care about. Once we shine a light on these fears, we often find that the monster in our closet is just a coat. Overcome your fears with the help of others.
-   Take someone you love with you and go do something you're afraid of. This could be simple fears like driving on the interstate or going to the movie theater, but it could also be a bigger issue like sitting in the waiting room for that doctor's appointment you've been putting off. Use support to help you achieve something that you've been dreading.
-   Share with someone about something you are afraid you will fail in. Let a loved one read that thing you wrote or hear the song you've been working on. Let a friend watch your presentation or tell them you have a plan to propose.

Lesson 6: joy is real (and it is different from happiness).

[13] May the God of hope fill you with all joy and peace in believing, so that you may abound in hope by the power of the Holy spirit.

- Romans 15:13

[28] And we know that for those who love God all things work together for good, for those who are called according to His purpose.

- Romans 8:28

Through the sunshine and the rain, even sorrow and pain, Jesus is still my comfort and guide.
And His love comforts me, and His grace has set me free.
And someday I shall stand by His side.
I am blessed. I am blessed. Everyday that I live I am blessed.
When I wake up in the morning, til I lay my head to rest, I am blessed. I am blessed.

- Gospel song

When I was 5 years old, my mother always told me that happiness was the key to life. When I went to school, they asked me what I wanted to be when I grew up. I wrote down 'happy'. They told me I didn't understand the assignment, and I told them they didn't understand life.

- John Lennon

Look at John Lennon, delivering a third-degree burn to his teacher. I highly doubt a five-year old was savvy enough for that response, but that is a quote he claimed. If I had been his teacher, I would've calmly responded, "Well, Mr. Lennon, you can inform your mother that she is mistaken. Happiness is an emotion contingent upon external circumstance. As such, a life spent in pursuit of happiness would be spent vainly attempting to control circumstances outside of ourselves. Thus, a life in search of happiness is destined for only frustration, despair, and failure." Burn returned. No five-year-old can hang with me. Or, maybe I would've just said, "Uh. Dang. That's good."

Being serious, that quote from John Lennon seems like a noble purpose for life, but as the fictitious me so eloquently explained, happiness should never be our goal. Happiness is always in response to something. I am happy because I got to eat ice cream. What about when I want ice cream and I don't get it? What am I then, unhappy? Happiness is a thermometer reacting to the environment. Joy is a thermostat controlling the environment. Joy is a choice. It is internal happiness that is not affected by external circumstances. True joy transcends the rolling waves of circumstance.

George's healthiest day still had more physical pain and struggle than my sickest. Everyone is happy when things go right. Everyone is loving when things are good. What if death had been lurking in the shadows your whole life and no moment had ever been completely free of struggle? Who would you be then? People flocked to George because he was joyful when he should've been bitter. He was loving when he should've harbored resentment. When you truly have love in your life, your thermostat is set to joy. Remember, to love is to show someone else their beauty, their worth, and their importance. It doesn't require receiving anything in return. Love is your choice. When you choose love, you are choosing to come from a mindset that looks for beauty in the world and in yourself. These things separate you from the world as a follower of Christ. Love doesn't just happen on Sunday or when everything is going well. Love happens when things are going wrong, when you're upset or depressed, when you have every reason to give up.

It sounds strange to suggest you can have joy when you are depressed. They are opposing emotions in every sense. Even so, true joy exists when you can look beyond this singular moment to the greater picture. I have suffered from depression for sixteen years. Many of those years were extremely dark times where there was no hope in my life. When my alarm would go off, I would lay in bed struggling to make myself get up. I would think, "I cannot lie to the world again today. I can't pretend to be okay." Eventually, I would drag myself out of bed, plaster on a smile, and trudge through my day. I would be so physically and mentally exhausted when I returned home that I would lay in bed the moment I got home and not get up again until the next morning to repeat the cycle. I still suffer from periods of depression today. There are still days when nothing has meaning and all I want to do is close myself off from the world. Even on those days, I understand that there is something to live for. I accept there is beauty in the world and that I add to that beauty. I can see beyond the current struggle to all the gifts I've been given. I can center my daily life around God, and I can live a life of joy even during my lowest days. That is the light Christ has given me. He also gives me an anchor to hold onto as life's stormy waters toss me back and forth with rocks that would break me on every side. He has given me peace within the storm, knowing that I have already won in this life and the next because I know there is something more. There is something beyond my depression. In that realization, my joy is mine and it cannot be taken away.

The lessons we have discussed so far become the natural byproduct of joy. When you have joy, you can have courage in the face of struggle. With joy, you have strength to continue to stand when there seems to be every reason to lie down. Joy provides us faith that there will be a way when there seems to be none. In joy, we realize that we don't need new revelations or gifts to overcome each problem. We just need the courage and self-discipline to hang on to the truth that the gifts we have already received are enough. We have been given the gift of life when we did nothing to deserve it. Every breath we breathe has been provided without a request for repayment. Joy is the ability to look at life through the eyes of gratitude. In our darkest of days, there is always light.

I want to take a brief break from George's story of joy to share one more lesson he taught me that feels appropriate here: wisdom. Having all of these attributes—courage, strength, faith, and joy—doesn't mean you will never face struggle. Loving God doesn't spare us from pain or sickness, it only gives us refuge in the storm. There is a time when it is appropriate to seek professional help to assist in your battle. George didn't face his health struggles alone. That would've universally been considered ludicrous. He wisely sought out medical help. He used his strength, courage, and faith to face life with joy in the interim while he held out for his healing.

For some reason, there is a social stigma that says we should not follow this same conventional wisdom in seeking out help for our mental health struggles. There seems to be the thought that if you are depressed, just be stronger or have more faith and you'll be fine. If you have anxiety, just have more courage, and it'll go away. This is preposterous, and I want to make sure you know that sort of thinking is not the point of this lesson. Just because these illnesses aren't visible doesn't make them any less real or have any less biological cause.

The devil's greatest lie is that you have to be more. You aren't enough to deserve Christ's love.

- o The scars on His hands say that is a lie.
- o The wounds on His head say you are enough.
- o The lashes on His back say you are worthy.
- o The hole in His side says you matter.
- o All of that was for you. Not for who you want to be, but for who you really are.

So, it doesn't matter if the whole world doesn't understand. Christ does. He sees you and loves you. We all face stress, but do not confuse stress with anxiety or depression. They are in no way the same thing. Yes, everyone deals with stress. No, everyone does not deal with depression or anxiety.

Even during the struggles that are to come later in my life, I have always dealt with stress admirably. Still, I almost threw my life away due to my refusal to speak out against my struggles with depression and anxiety in fear of what others may think of me. If you are struggling, use wisdom and get the medical interventions that are available. Do not suffer needlessly and in silence. Be brave enough to reach out for help. Be a part of the solution that breaks this stigma and saves millions of us from pain and heartache that could easily be avoided.

And now, back to our regularly scheduled programming.

George had never gone on a vacation because he had to stay near his doctor in case of a medical emergency, but in July of 2004 George's health was as good as ever. As a celebration, my parents, brother, and I took George to the beach for the first time in his life. Since it is the closest beach to our home in Kentucky, we decided to travel to Myrtle Beach. The first day of our trip, George was as happy as I ever saw him. He reveled in the fact that he was able to wakeboard as good or better than any of us. He was never bashful to do a little trash talking. The day was filled with laughter and love. That night, George, my brother, and I sat on our hotel's balcony watching the waves roll in. We reminisced of the fun of the day and cherished our opportunity to be together. As the night waned on, conversation began to naturally fade. My brother eventually went to bed while George and I continued to watch the ocean in silence. Just as I was about to head in for the night, George quietly began to speak. He wasn't really looking at me or even seeming to speak to me at all. Instead, it felt like he was just thinking aloud. He only said one sentence. "I don't see how anyone could look at beauty like this and question if there is a God."

He wasn't focused on the fact that he was twenty-nine years old and only visiting the beach for the first time. He didn't dwell on the undeniable reality that his momentary health was only a reprieve from the inevitable return of his struggles. He didn't care that Myrtle Beach is at the top of no one's list of pristine beaches. His focus was on today, not yesterday or tomorrow. He was alive in the moment. He was loving life, relishing the beauty that God has given us all. It was the definition of joy. It had been ten years since his transplant. Even though he had already doubled the maximum life expectancy of patients receiving a triple transplant at the time, he seemed more stable than usual. Doctors continued to speculate about how much time he had left, but that wasn't nothing new for us. It had been ten years since his transplant, and he was healthier than ever. He had already doubled the maximum lifespan expected after a transplant like his. This was surprising to no one who knew him. We were all excited for many more years together.

Joy Action Challenge

- Look around. Open your eyes. Not figuratively, literally. Actually look around and see the beauty in the world. Describe the beauty of what you see. If you don't run out of room to write with an extensive list still waiting to be detailed, then open your eyes wider. Beauty is all around us. Set your thermostat to joy. Look for it. Spread it. Enjoy life.

Lifestyle change:

Life is not meant to be lived alone. Joy is meant to be shared. Enjoy life today with the people you care about the most. Put aside your worries and fears for a day of pure peace and contentment. Spend time basking in the gifts of each other and the world.

Lesson 7: goodbye is real (and one day it will be forever).

[18] *For I know that good itself does not dwell in me, that is, in my sinful nature. For I have the desire to do what is good, but I cannot carry it out.* [19] *For I do not do the good I want to do, but the evil I do not want to do—this I keep on doing.*
- *Romans 7:18-19*

I know your life on Earth was troubled.
And only you could know the pain.
You weren't afraid to face the devil,
You were no stranger to rain.
Go rest high on that mountain.
Son, your work on Earth is done.
Go to heaven a-shoutin' love for the Father and the Son
- *"Go Rest High on That Mountain" by Vince Gill*

Maybe time running out is a gift
I'll work hard 'til the end of my shift
And give you every second I can find
And hope it isn't me who's left behind
- *"If We Were Vampires" by Jason Isbell* ← *greatest singer/songwriter of all time (only my opinion...but, still, a fact)*

[13] *Now listen, you who say, "Today or tomorrow we will go to this or that city, spend a year there, carry on business and make money." Why, you do not even know what will happen tomorrow. What is your life? You are a mist that appears for a little while and then vanishes. Instead, you ought to say, "If it is the Lord's will, we will live and do this or that."*
- *James 4:13-15*

I wanted to let out everything I had held inside my whole life there on that balcony in Myrtle Beach. I wanted to tell George everything he meant to me. I wanted to tell him that all of his pain wasn't in vain. I longed for him to understand that my life was better because of his struggles. All of our lives were. We wanted to be strong because he was strong. We wanted to be good because he was good. We wanted to love because he loved.

I wanted to tell him I loved him. Not just the words "I love you" that are sometimes empty but that I loved him with everything in me. With every ounce of me, I love you. I love you more than I know how to tell you. I love you more than I can describe. There is not a single decision I make that isn't impacted by you in some way.

I'm crying as I write. I've cried again and again and again as I've relived this moment throughout my life. But, on that July night in 2004, I was nineteen years old. I was the age George was when he was brave enough to risk his life to have his transplant. But I wasn't brave enough to cry. He was my hero. My everything. I wanted him to think I was strong. I wanted him to think I was brave. To keep from crying, I said nothing. We sat there in silence for a while longer before he turned in for bed.

We finished out the vacation with more laughs and love. Everything in the world was good. Toward the end of the trip, George's feet began to swell up. This was such a small issue compared to what he usually faced that we barely even registered it. It was to be expected that his feet would swell after being so active all week. I didn't know at the time that his heart was beginning to fail. It wasn't pumping hard enough to move the blood out of his feet and up through his body against gravity. Fluid was accumulating in his feet because his heart was shutting down. It was a signal for the beginning of the end.

A week later we were back in Kentucky after our vacation. The rest of my family was in our hometown of Clay County, and I was in Lexington for college. I got the call to come back home because George was dying. He had suffered another heart attack, and there didn't seem to be a way through this time. I drove from Lexington back to Manchester, but I honestly was only moderately alarmed. It didn't matter if there was no way he could survive, he would anyway. When I got to the hospital, George was hooked up to a ventilator to keep him alive. There were wires running in and out of his body. Everyone in our family was there crying, comforting each other.

The doctor at the Manchester Emergency room sent George to St. Joseph's Hospital in Lexington by ambulance. He told my mother to be prepared because George may not make it to Lexington. Even so, by the next day, George seemed to have pulled through again and was off the ventilator. He had overcome a doctor's belief that his death was imminent just like he always did. Just like I knew he would. He began progressing back toward health, or whatever qualified as health for him.

Much of our family were mainstays in the St. Joseph Hospital lobby. We ate there. We slept there. We lived there. This wasn't a new experience for us. The hospital had been filled with our family for days. The hospital employees allowed us to stretch the visitor limitations because they all adored George. When he was on the ventilator and couldn't speak, he would shake their hands to show them thanks. After he could again speak, he was his thoughtful self again as he spent most of his time checking on all of us rather than showing concern for himself.

After three days of living at the hospital, we all needed a change of clothes and personal items from home. Everyone was certain of his progression toward health and planned to return immediately the next day. Only five of us remained at the hospital: George's parents, my brother, my sister-in-law, and me. After everyone left, I went in to check on Bubby and spend some time with him in his room. For one of the only times I can ever remember, he wasn't smiling and upbeat. I could tell he was in a deeply introspective moment. Being nineteen years old, instead of respecting his privacy, I asked what he was thinking about. He told me what the doctor who had been leaving as I was coming into the room had told him: they could continue to put him on a ventilator and bring him back after his heart attacks, but his heart had deteriorated to the point where they could no longer prevent the heart attacks from occurring. He told George that he had to decide when he was becoming a burden on his family. In other words, he was suggesting that it was time to decide whether the next heart attack should be his last. I was infuriated. I exclaimed that the doctor had no idea what George meant to our family and that he had no right to insinuate that George could ever be a burden on us. At that point, Bubby shrugged off the doctor's comments as meaningless and transitioned back to the man I always knew him to be. The most loving, courageous, strong man I have ever known. My hero.

What I didn't know and couldn't understand at the time was that the doctor's comments had not simply faded away as I thought. They had taken root. Months before, he had talked to my mom about not being placed back on life support. When he had his severe heart attack in our hometown, my mom said it was the first time she had ever seen him afraid. When the doctors came into the ER, George softly asked for them to help him. After the doctor had mentioned that he was becoming a burden on his family, George had decided he would never go back on life support again.

The next morning, George was being moved from one bed to another so he could be taken for more tests. This slight activity spurred another major heart attack. This time, he refused to let them put him back on a ventilator. This time, he chose that it was his time to go. He chose, as the doctor had gracelessly put it, to no longer be a burden on his family. Those of us who had remained at the hospital stood helplessly beside the bed as the greatest person any of us would ever know left this world. I wanted to scream at the top of my lungs. I wanted to beg him not to give up. I wanted to plead for him to just fight because I knew he would come through again. We would have more time together. I wanted to beg him to stay. I wanted to let him know that he was the reason for everything good in me. I wanted to tell him that I couldn't do this without him. I couldn't live without him. I had always lived my life trying to be who he'd want me to be, and, without him, I just didn't know who I was.

I wanted to say all the things I almost said two weeks ago on that balcony in Myrtle Beach, but it was too late. They had given him morphine to help him slip away more peacefully. Instead of saying anything, I just stood there and wept. The tears I had always been afraid to show him during his life flowed and flowed during his death. And sixteen years later, they've never really stopped. Not inside. A part of me has never left that hospital bed.

Goodbye Action Challenge

I lied to you in the Author's Notes section (because it's always good to base a relationship off of a lie). I claimed that I had done all of these action challenges. I have done them all. All except this one. This one, I ran out of time to do. There is nothing in my life I wouldn't give to be able to do this challenge, but George is gone. I'd wrap my arms around him. I wouldn't be ashamed of the tears. I'd say that all the pain you went through wasn't in vain. It was for me. My life is better because of you. My daughter's life is better because of you. Everything good in me is because I believe it is what you'd have me to be. This book is for you. My life has been lived in your honor.

I'd say all those things, but he's not here to hear them. He never will be again. This is the only regret in my life I can't redeem. The only thing I cannot fix. That night in Myrtle Beach was just the last time that I almost told him but didn't. It certainly wasn't the only time. It was just the last instance of me deciding that tomorrow would be the day. Tomorrow, I will tell him. So many times in a moment of emotional bravery I picked up the phone to call him only to set it back down and resolve that today wasn't the right day. Tomorrow most definitely would be. No doubt about it. Tomorrow, I will tell him. He will know. Just not today. Eventually, I ran out of tomorrows. I ran out of chances.

- List the people you hold most dear, the people you love the most.

Lifestyle change:

If you don't make a single change in your life, I beg you at least do this one. Run to the people you love and tell them today, not tomorrow. Through the lifestyle changes we've gone through already, you should've already done this. Have you been putting it off? This very second, reach out to the people you listed above and let them know what they mean to you. Don't just say "I love you" and move along. Make sure they know you mean it. Tell them not only that you love them but the depths to which you do so. Remember, to love is to show another the beauty of themselves. Let them know how much they matter and how much they've meant to your life. And, not just in words but in action. Don't put this off. If you aren't willing to do it today, you won't be willing to do it tomorrow. If you leave this challenge undone, I promise you that one day you will wish you hadn't.

Lesson 8: regret is real (and it can destroy your life).

[20] *The one who sins is the one who will die. The child will not share the guilt of the parent, nor will the parent share the guilt of the child. The righteousness of the righteous will be credited to them, and the wickedness of the wicked will be charged against them.*

- Ezekiel 18:20

Spend all your time waiting for that second chance
For a break that would make it okay. There's always some reason
To feel not good enough, and it's hard at the end of the day.
I need some distraction. Oh, beautiful release.
Memories seep from my veins, let me be empty.
Oh, and weightless, and maybe I'll find some peace tonight.
In the arms of the angel fly away from here.
From this dark, cold, hotel room and the endlessness that you fear.
You are pulled from the wreckage of your silent reverie.
You're in the arms of the angel may you find some comfort here.
So tired of the straight line and everywhere you turn.
There's vultures and thieves at your back. The storm keeps on twisting.
Keep on building the lies that you make up for all that you lack.
It don't make no difference. Escaping one last time.
It's easier to believe in this sweet madness. Oh, this glorious sadness that brings me to my knees.
In the arms of the angel fly away from here.
From this dark, cold, hotel room and the endlessness that you fear.
You are pulled from the wreckage of your silent reverie.
You're in the arms of the angel may you find some comfort here

- "Angel" by Sarah McLachlan

George had always wished he was a great singer. Once, he said he had a dream where he was at a funeral singing "Angel" by Sarah McLachlan. He talked about how beautiful his voice sounded. He said when he looked down he saw himself in the casket. His dream got most of the story right. The song was sung at his funeral and it was beautiful, but it was performed by one of my best friends. Years later, I will sing that song to Georgia every night as I rock her to sleep. I'll tell her about her Bubby George, and why her name is the most special name in the whole world. I'll tell her how he touched so many lives and that she is going to change the world just like him. And every time I sing her this song it will serve as reminder that if I had been more, I wouldn't have to tell her about him. He'd still be living so she could see for herself.

George's funeral was held in our hometown of Manchester, KY. At this funeral home, there are two rooms available where two separate ceremonies can be held. At George's funeral, both rooms had to be reserved because so many people were in attendance. The room where his body lay was standing room only. The line to view his body extended into the lobby and continued into the secondary room. The line wound throughout the funeral home until literally no other people could enter so it ended out in the parking lot.

I was one of the pallbearers, so I was seated in the front row directly by the exit door. All of these people, hundreds of them, walked by me on their way out. They all stopped to express their sympathy for my family. Each one had a different story to tell of how George impacted their life and had meant so much to them. Many of these stories told of instances that were seemingly so small. The way he made them feel loved in the smallest moments. The way he made them feel worthy and beautiful.

These stories were recounted to me as their way of honoring the life that had meant so much to so many. Yet they meant nothing to me. Each time, I would just tell them, "Thank you for coming." I was trying to be respectful and appreciative. Hundreds of times, again and again, "Thank you for coming." I can still hear my voice repeating that phrase in a robotic monotone. "Thank you for coming." "Thank you for coming."

All the while, in my mind, my thoughts were bitter. "This is my fault. I am guilty, but you are all accomplices. I don't need to hear what he meant to you. He needed to hear it. He would've never believed that doctor when he insinuated that he was a burden on others if even just one of you would have told him what he meant to you. When he went to sleep alone in his bed at his mom and dad's house, he needed to hear it. When he didn't get to walk at his high school graduation like everyone else, he needed to hear it. When he had a teacher in college who was failing him because of excessive absences, not caring that the absences were due to extended stints in the hospital, George needed it. He had a B average in her class and was in the hospital facing death at the time of finals, but his teacher didn't want to give him the option to make up the final. When he had other people trying to limit his life and his future even beyond what his health did, he needed us. When he had to accept he would never be able to pursue a real career or his passions, he needed it. You can save your well wishes. I don't need or want them."

I knew what that doctor had told him and what George had believed. He had to choose when he no longer wanted to be a burden on people. Ultimately, George chose July 14, 2004. If I had told him what he meant to me that night in Myrtle Beach, he could have never believed he was a burden. He would've known he was the anchor of my life. It was my fault, and it was theirs. It was everyone who ever knew him. He gave us all so much. He touched all of us in so many ways, but we took that gift and never bothered to repay it. We were all too consumed with our own lives to give back to the person who gave us so much. We were all too obtuse to realize that just because he never asked for anything in return didn't mean he actually lacked the need for it.

He was strong for all of us, but none of us were strong for him. He showed us what it meant to have joy, but when his joy started to falter, none of us were there to show him support. He lived courageously and inspired us to live courageously in return. Still, no one bothered to tell him that his courage made their life better. He lived a life of faith to the very last second. All of us showed up at the funeral to honor that life. We all told each other how we were able to fight through fear in our lives because we never saw him buckle in the face of perceivably unclimbable mountains of hopelessness. We hugged each other and shared stories of his influence out in the parking lot because he touched so many of us.

We just all forgot to bother to tell him. I hated them all for that.

Most of all, I hated myself. I had spent my whole life trying to be for everybody else who he was for me. I don't remember a time when I didn't try to be strong when someone else needed me or stand beside someone courageously when they struggled to stand alone. I tried to be George for everyone else, but when he needed someone like himself, I let him down. Ultimately, it was my responsibility. They weren't there the night he let his guard down in Myrtle Beach to show vulnerability and tenderness. They weren't with him in the hospital while he tried to process what the doctor had just told him. I was.

At the funeral and for the next thirteen years, I lived knowing that I killed him. He chose to go, but he chose to go because of me. Nothing could have taken him if he had kept fighting. He just decided it was time for the fight to end. And, he made that decision because I had failed to let him know that he shouldn't. I had silenced my desire to let him know he wasn't fighting a pointless battle alone. His life-long fight had been for all of us. The victory was the lives—the joy, faith, strength, and courage—he gave all of us.

Life went on without him, but it didn't really. Not for me anyway. I continued to live the same life, but for much different reasons. I was still giving and loving. I still put others first, but now I did it because I felt like I had to, not because I got to. I kept living like he did because he deserved for me to. I kept trying to be George for the rest of the world. Even though I succeeded in this goal for many of them, I never did in my own head.

Inside, darkness began to spread. I never told anyone about that night in Myrtle Beach or what the doctor had told him. No one but me knew my responsibility in his death. I carried my shame and guilt alone. I never told anyone because I knew how much he meant to them. I didn't want them to know that if it wasn't for me, he'd still be here.

George's favorite verse was Matthew 17:20: "Truly I tell you, if you have faith as small as a mustard seed, you can say to this mountain, 'Move from here to there,' and it will move. Nothing will be impossible for you." He kept that faith his whole life. He never gave up hope that his miracle would come. Mark 4:30-32 says, "[30] And He said, 'How shall we picture the kingdom of God, or by what parable shall we present it? [31] It is like a mustard seed, which, when sown upon the soil, though it is smaller than all the seeds that are upon the soil, [32] yet when it is sown, it grows up and becomes larger than all the garden plants and forms large branches; so that the birds of the air can nest under its shade."

Faith had been his mustard seed. Personal resentment was mine. It started small and grew and grew. I took my blessings of great role-models and made them my curse. To pay respect to them, I had to be perfect. Nonetheless, I knew that when the real tests of life came, I would fail. If I couldn't be enough for him, the person I loved more than anyone else in the world, I couldn't be enough for anybody. I knew I was a fraud because I acted like him, but I was not. I thought because I could handle my pain, I should. I internalized it all. All the guilt. All the shame. I just swallowed it, put my head down, and kept going.

He was the anchor to all that was good in me. Without him, I drifted out into a sea of darkness, untethered to all I had ever known about the world or myself. I had no more hope. I had no more faith. I struggled for so long to get back to shore, but I could not swim. Every time I would go under the water and fear I'd never surface again, I'd remember him and struggle back up for one more breath. And so I continued for thirteen years. Drowning but not calling out for help. Dying each day in silence.

Regret Action Challenge

- Revisit your greatest failure from our first action challenge, but this time I want us to look at it from a broader perspective. Instead of looking at the days and weeks after it, I want to look at the months and years that followed. What regrets do you have surrounding that situation?

- Describe how you have moved on (or failed to move on) from that situation.

- How has that failure impacted the rest of your life?

Lifestyle change:

Are you still in that place of failure? Have you given up hope of ever leaving it? I stayed there for thirteen years. I was still beside his bed wanting to beg him not to go. It seemed the longer time went on, the less of me there was left. A little piece of me drifted away each day until all that was left was a hollow shell of who I could have been. Don't let the same thing happen to you. The only medicine for this shame is vulnerability. You have to open up and let the love of others in. You have to accept that their love for you is unconditional and persists even in your failures. Today, when you are with the people who care about you, allow yourself to actually feel their love. Let it shine a light on the darkness within.

I know some of you may not feel like anyone is showing

you love. My heart goes out to you because I know that makes your recovery so much more difficult, but you need to remember what love is. Love is to show someone their beauty, their worth, and their importance. If you feel like love is lacking in your life, go make it become a reality. Show yourself that you are beautiful, important, and worthy. You be the spark that lights the fire of love in your life. Once you begin loving others, I assure you the most natural thing in the world is for them to start loving you back.

This is also the secret for accepting that the people who love you do so unconditionally. A lot of the people you are trying to show love will have messed up. Some of them will have made terrible mistakes, but they still deserve love. And, if they do, you do too. No matter how you've messed up, there is still love in the world for you.

Part 3: Meet my dad, Tim Reid, who taught me...

My dad, Tim Reid, and mom, Pat Reid

Dad preaching at his church, Morgan Branch Pentecostal

Me (left), Dad (middle), and Alan, my brother (right)

Mom and Dad's wedding

George in my dad's words[3]:

- *George would get mad when Pat didn't want us to just stay at home with them. He said she was hogging me.*
- *I remember running with George on my back. He loved it. One day, we challenged Dave and Bill to a race with me running with George. As I ran, George was calling, "Come on guys, you can catch us. Don't give up." He told me when I ran with him, it felt like he was running by himself.*
- *I loved all three of the boys (George, Dave, and Bill), and they became my boys.*
- *Remember to enjoy everyday events. They can offer you a lifetime of laughter and memories.*

Lifestyle Change: Find the laughter in life. You're about to read about a man who worked more than any other person I've ever met. He was constantly exhausted and sacrificed himself for others at every opportunity. Yet his love of life remained and was contagious. He spread cheer everywhere he went, in the good times and bad. Finding the laughter in your life won't just brighten your day; it will brighten the days of everyone you meet.

---

[3] *My uncle George was a man who changed many lives, not just mine. He lived and loved in a way that was truly unique. For Christmas the year our daughter Georgia was born, my ex-wife Hope gave me a gift I cherish. She had George's friends and family write a letter to Georgia answering the question, "Who was George West to you?" These letters are meant for Georgia to know why her name is so special even though she never met the man who inspired it. From here on, each part of the book begins with a section titled "George in Their Own Words" containing excerpts from that person's letter. There is also a section in the appendix with many more responses of people explaining how George impacted their lives.*

Lesson 9: servant leadership is real (and the value of family).

43 Not so with you. Instead, whoever wants to become great among you must be your servant, 44 and whoever wants to be first must be slave of all. 45 For even the Son of Man did not come to be served, but to serve, and to give his life as a ransom for many.

- Mark 10:43-45

16 All Scripture is God-breathed and is useful for teaching, rebuking, correcting and training in righteousness.

- 2 Timothy 3:16

31 For I swear, dear brothers and sisters, that I face death daily. This is as certain as my pride in what Christ Jesus our Lord has done in you.

- 1 Corinthians 15:31

35 In all things I have shown you that by working hard in this way we must help the weak and remember the words of the Lord Jesus, how He himself said, "It is more blessed to give than receive."

- Acts 20:35

I'm thirty-five years old, and I still sometimes struggle to be an adult. My dad has been an adult since he was a boy.

Every day of school my dad attended in his life was followed immediately by going to work. His father had a furniture company, and Dad began working there when he was six years old. His duties weren't just small tasks to humor a kid, letting him play while the adults worked. When he was six years old, he would clean the floors, stuff the couch backs with padding, and draw the patterns for the furniture the factory made. He was legitimately working. My daughter is six years old, and she asked that I not get her any toys that made her run last Christmas because she's too lazy.

Dad's responsibilities and work hours increased as he grew older. He started helping load and unload the furniture for deliveries when he was ten or eleven years old. He worked there until the factory burned down when he was fourteen.

After the factory burned, his dad, Shirley Don Reid, bought coal trucks. My dad was trained to be the main mechanic. He worked six days a week, often more than forty hours. They owned five trucks which would typically quit hauling around 11:00 p.m. When the trucks came in for the night, he had to change the tires and do any necessary mechanical check-up. If a truck had significant problems, he would work well into the early morning, go home to shower, and head to school with little to no sleep. He began periodically driving the trucks when he was fifteen years old to haul dirt and coal. When I was fifteen, I was searching my armpits to count my six underarm hairs and bask in my manliness.

Dad was not permitted to study or do schoolwork unless he was caught up in the garage and waiting for the next truck to come in. I'm not trying to villainize my grandparents. They are wonderful people who loved my dad. They were poor and needed everyone working together to get by. Still, it became impossible to succeed in both work and school. There was really no choice when it came to which arena would receive his focus and care. Consequently, his schoolwork suffered. My dad was struggling to read and failed English for a semester his junior year. He ultimately followed in the footsteps of the other men in his family as both of his older brothers had quit school and gone to work without graduating.

He and my mom started dating the year Dad dropped out. Although only two months apart in age, my mom was a year ahead of him in school because he had been held back after his eighth-grade year. He asked for her hand in marriage in May of 1982. My mother, who had just graduated high school, had been eighteen for three months while my dad, who was to be a senior, had been eighteen for less than a month. My dad is a highly intelligent man who had a natural knack for mathematics, but his knowledge was never developed through school. My dad was never paid to work while he was a student, so after asking my mom to marry him, he decided to drop out of school to be paid $100 a week for six days of work at the garage. This decision, made while he was still a kid, would impact the rest of his life. My mom and dad were married on July 24, 1982. At eighteen years old, I was sleeping too late to get up for 11:00 a.m. classes.

When my dad was eighteen, he became the leader of our family and took on the responsibilities that came with that distinction.

Dad dedicated his life to providing for us with the limited opportunities his lack of education provided him. He put aside any personal dreams or aspirations he may have ever had. Even though my dad loves to fish, I can count on two hands the number of times I remember him ever going. He worked over eighty hours a week hauling coal for the next twenty-eight years. As a coal truck driver, you only get paid for the loads you haul, not the hours you work. There are only so many hours in a day and, as such, only so many round trips he could make. Dad would leave at 1:30 a.m. to have his truck in the front of the line to begin the day's loads. He would be one of the last men still on the road each night, generally returning home between 6:00 and 8:00 p.m. after a fourteen to sixteen-hour workday. He never worked less than a twelve-hour day the entire time I was growing up. He has told my mom that he would be exhausted, but they would offer him another load. He would think to himself, "That load is Girlfriend (what he has always called my mom) another purse, or it's my boys another pair of shoes." So, he would keep on going. Truck drivers had no benefits, no vacation or sick time, no retirement. If his truck broke down, he didn't get paid, so he also spent time making sure it was properly maintained.

It wasn't just his time that Dad sacrificed. He literally worked his life away. The lifestyle of a coal truck driver contributed greatly to the development of his Type 2 Diabetes. He has had multiple heart attacks. There have been times we feared we may be saying goodbye to our leader for good. Last week, he completely lost vision in his left eye due to complications with diabetes. A few days ago, he received an injection directly into his eye in an attempt to recover his sight. We are praying for God to move on yet another miracle for our family. Simply put, my dad will die a younger man because of his sacrifice for us. He loved us more than he loved himself. He has given until he literally has no more to give.

Yet, somehow, he avoided the trap so many fall into while striving to provide for the ones they love. Even though he worked so much, it was clear to us all that we were the number one priority in his life. He wouldn't just be at all of the games Alan and I had when we were playing sports, he would coach our teams. He would show up at practice in his coal truck because he would come directly from work. He'd be in his work clothes, covered in oil serving as an assistant grade school football coach. He didn't have the time to do that, but he found the time anyway. I always knew that he sacrificed because of me and his love for us all. When he was home, he was truly home. He cherished our time together.

Many people seek leadership positions today but have no idea what a leader is. They long for the status and acclaim but have no interest in self-sacrifice. They confuse being a leader with having people serve you when in fact leadership means that you serve all. For my dad, it wasn't just the work hours he put in, it was his life. In every decision, we came first. In fact, when it came to himself or his family, it was no decision at all.

Servant Leadership Action Challenge

- Do you serve in any leadership roles, either as a parent, in the community, in your profession, or in any facet of your life? List the arenas where you are a leader. Describe how you approach your responsibilities in this role and your relationship with those who you lead.

- Look back over your descriptions from above. If I asked the people you lead what type of leader you are, would their responses match yours? Do you dedicate your time as their leader for their good or for your own? How do you think others would describe you as their leader?

Lifestyle Change:

Do your daily actions back up the leader you claim to be? How do your actions show those you lead their beauty, their worth, and their importance? You may feel that is too extreme if your leadership role is in the workforce or with non-family members. If you approach your leadership with that mindset, then you are their leader in title alone. To be invested in their leader, people must first know their leader is invested in them. Lead them by serving them. Don't do this out of duty but because you truly want the best for them. Lead with laughter and joy. When you, as the leader, lead with laughter and cheer, everyone else will follow. Within the next month, I want you to plan and implement an act of service that gives back to the individuals you lead. Even if you don't know what you will do yet, set a date. If you don't, this will get buried under other items on your to-do list. Go beyond what is expected of you to show your authentic appreciation.

Lesson 10: integrity is real (and the value of un-instagramming your life).

[1] Be careful not to practice your righteousness in front of others to be seen by them. If you do, you will have no reward from your Father in heaven.

- Matthew 6:1

Character may be manifested in the great moments, but it is made in the small ones.
- Phillips Brooks, Clergyman and author

Integrity is what you do when no one is watching; it's doing the right thing all of the time, even when it may work to your disadvantage.
- Uncommon by Tony Dungy

There's only one thing I hate more than lying: skim milk. Which is water that's lying about being milk.
- Ron Swanson

Don't call what you're wearing an outfit.
Don't ever say your car is broke.
Don't sing with a fake British accent.
Don't act like your family's a joke.
- "Outfit" by Drive-By Truckers

My dad was born April 24, 1964. My older brother was born on February 18th, one week to the day after my mom's birthday of February 11th. After my older brother, they realized they could do better so they decided to have me. I started my lifetime of showing him up by outdoing his birthday proximity. I was born April 24, 1985 on my dad's twenty-first birthday. Once I was born, it was obvious they had perfected creating a child, so they decided to call it quits. I'm pretty sure that was the primary reason, but a secondary, less significant reason was that the difficult childbirth almost killed my mother and me. The umbilical cord became entangled around my neck and was suffocating me. I was born black and blue with my heartbeat so weak it was barely perceptible. My parents were told there was a real chance I wouldn't survive and that if I did, I would be mentally and physically disabled. My dad prayed to God to save my life and pleaded that this would be the only birthday gift he would ever ask for. I believe God hears all prayers, but my dad seems to have a direct line to God's ear. As He always seems to do, God answered Dad's prayer and gave me the gift of a healthy life.

When Dad was sixteen years old, he walked to a church by himself. Back then Dad still had a good heart, but he had a terrible temper. He lost control of himself and would fight often. He didn't bully others, but he has said he literally enjoyed fighting. He knew something was missing in his life. He was emotionally distant from others. Up until that day, he had told two people—his mother and his granny—that he loved them. That day, God called on his heart so he went to the altar, but he didn't know how to pray. He just cried out, "Jesus. Jesus. Help me Jesus." A woman at the church knelt to pray with him and told him, "Son, that's the way." My dad arose from the altar on his way to becoming the most loving man I have ever met.

The responsibilities of work and family had inadvertently caused Dad to grow distant in his relationship with God until I was born. My parents went to Sunday School sporadically but not consistently enough to truly influence their lives. Dad told Mom he wanted to give his very best to his sons, but without God in his life he couldn't be the father we deserved. He wanted to be an example for us boys of a man who is dedicated to God. He rededicated his life to God on June 23rd, 1985.

My papaw knew the strength of Dad's dedication and leadership. They each drove coal trucks and worked together daily. Dad knew just how sick Papaw truly was as he was losing his battle with diabetes, but he asked my dad not to let the rest of the family know. Even though Dad was the middle child, Papaw told him that he would be the next leader of the family. Papaw died on November 13th, 1988 at forty-eight years old. My father was only twenty-four.

Papaw had inadvertently placed a heavy burden on my dad by asking him to keep the severity of his health problems a secret. Dad experienced guilt and hopelessness as he searched for a way to ease the pain of his family. He spiraled into one of the darkest periods of his life. He barely slept. His parents' home was directly down the hill from ours. Dad would get up at night and look out the window to see his mom's lights on late into the night as she suffered alone. He struggled to help himself, but even more damning were his impotent attempts to shelter everyone else, especially my mamaw, from their pain. He had lost the joy in his life. Even though he was the middle child of five, he felt like he had to be the father and protector for all of his brothers and his sister. He thought he needed to have enough strength not only for himself but for everyone else as well. He became bitter at God as he suffered from undiagnosed depression, just as I did. He put on a happy face to everyone, just as I would do sixteen years later. My mom knew he was struggling, but she didn't realize the depth of his despair. Like me, he hid his struggles from the world out of both pride and an attempt to protect the ones he loved. Feelings of inadequacy are natural as you try hopelessly to make everyone else's pain go away.

My dad was hurting beyond his ability to bear. For one year, four months, and seventeen days he struggled with deep depression. He finally reached a breaking point and prayed to God, telling Him he could no longer take it. He told God that night if He couldn't deliver him from the state he was in, then to just forget him altogether. I know that seems like an extremely harsh reaction toward God, but Dad had literally come to the end of his strength.

That night, God answered his prayer. My dad dreamed he was at his parents' house talking with his mom about his dad. The back door opened, and he got up to see his father coming in. He met him in the kitchen and hugged him. His dad looked like a healthy, young man as he appeared in his army pictures from his twenties. He told my mamaw he needed to tell Tim something. He got my dad by the hand and placed his left hand on Dad's shoulder. He said, "Son, hold on. Heaven is worth everything. Heaven is worth everything." He then turned to leave. My dad tried to get him to stop, but Papaw told him he had to go. He stopped at the door, turned around, and said for the third time, "Heaven is worth everything." Then, he walked back out the door. My dad then woke up. His depression, anger, and anxiety were instantly gone. He has never suffered from them again.

My dad was renewed with a desire to make it to heaven more than anything. Seeing his dad's hands without wrinkles and without being worn from work had inspired him. He was reinvigorated by his dad's bright, pearly smile and seeing his body without injury, sickness, or pain. He never grieved over his loss to those depths again. His vision changed him forever as it put a desire for Heaven in him that has never dimmed.

I guess my only exceptional trait has been my ability early on to recognize how lucky I was to have George and Dad in my life. I've had an innate drive to be good because of it and the grit to keep going regardless of how dire my situation has gotten. Even as a child, I understood the sacrifices both made and that by the world's standards their lives hadn't amounted to much. One was a man who worked double the hours I worked as a teacher and made less money (and trust me, I didn't make a lot of money). The other was a man who most people defined by his illness. Even so, they had something more valuable than public acclaim. They had authenticity. They were real. They lived lives that backed up their words.

The only man I've ever known my father to be is the joyful, love-filled person who walked away from that vision. I do not recall in detail a single sermon I ever heard my dad preach (and I have heard over a thousand). Not one. What I do remember is who he was everyday. I've had several people tell me he was the same man when they saw him covered in oil driving a coal truck as he was behind a pulpit. The lessons of my life came from his living, not his lectures. They came from his practice, not his preaching. My dad didn't boast about his diligent prayer life, but if he had, it would not be the reason I believe prayer is real. I believe prayer is real because we didn't have a lot of money growing up. When I got sick, my parents couldn't afford to take me to the doctor. I remember waking up in the middle of the night with tear drops falling on my feet as my dad prayed for my healing. Years later when I struggled with alcohol, my dad never once told me what I was doing was wrong. I knew it was wrong because of the life he lived and the example he had set. It didn't matter that he was a pastor or that lots of people turned to him. What mattered was who he was as a man. I saw love in his life every day. I saw the joy I did not have. He didn't need to broadcast to the world who he was. Anyone who spent more than five minutes with him already knew.

I have always had the desire to live my life in a way that made their lives worth it. Even as a kid, I tried to live with the integrity I saw in them. I got in five fights my first five days of kindergarten. I was the smallest kid in class, boy or girl, and the biggest kid in class figured I'd be the easiest person to bully. On day one, he bullied me, so I fought him (and lost). The next day, he still had some bullying in his system but must've not felt like beating me up again so he decided to bully someone else. On day two, I fought him for bullying another kid (and I lost again). This kid must have come into school with his bullying tank filled to the brim because this cycle repeated for three more days. He would bully some other kid, and I would fight him again (and lose again). (Side note, where were the teachers at recess? Seems like after four days of the same kids fighting you'd keep them separated on the fifth day.) Mom says the next Monday after the sixth day of school I came home exclaiming that I hadn't even gotten into a fight that day. I was so proud. I guess he didn't want to fight me anymore, so he left everyone alone. Too bad too because I was just sizing him up the first five times. I would've had him right where I wanted him for number six. I'm like Rocky but this time the ref called the fight after Apollo Creed pummeled me for the first five rounds.

I wasn't fighting this kid repeatedly because I enjoyed getting beaten up. I definitely wasn't fighting him for how it would look to everyone else as I don't believe being known as the kid who gets beaten up every day wins you any popularity contest. I was fighting him because I thought standing up for myself and others was the right thing to do, and I have seen the men in my life do the right thing no matter the cost.

Integrity Action Challenge
- Make a list of five good things you've done in the last month.

In this book, there will be a lot more talk of all the ways I screwed up than the few good deeds I sprinkled in along the way. Any positive action on my end that I do discuss here is most often to highlight the greatness and worth of someone else. Any act of kindness I've done in my life isn't for me or for you. It was for that person in that moment. I know this comes off as self-righteous. It feels self-righteous writing it. Even so, I don't want this book to perpetuate what I see as a virus destroying our society. So many people are consumed by doing the right thing but for the wrong reasons.

- Examine each of the good deeds you listed above separately. Circle the deed if you DID NOT: a) do it in front of other people, b) know that other people would find out about it, or c) do something to make sure other people heard about it. Of your five good acts, how many are circled?
- Obviously if you do enough positive stuff, people are going to know about some of them. You shouldn't avoid doing kind things just because other people will know. I'm just saying you shouldn't do it only because they will know. Examine your motives and be honest with yourself. What is your inspiration for your good deeds? Are you doing the right things for the right reasons? Would you be satisfied if you never received notoriety for your deeds?

Lifestyle change:

This is going to step on some toes and that's fine. If you do something good and your first instinct is to get on Facebook to tell everyone about it, then you shouldn't do it at all. Everyone involved would be better off. That isn't love. It's a farce masquerading as love and only serves to perpetuate the shallowness that consumes many of us. You aren't showing that person the beauty of themselves. You are showing the world the beauty of you. There's no real enjoyment from this. It's hollow. Tomorrow, do something for someone else and just enjoy yourself in the moment. Laugh together. Live together. Let that be enough for you.

Don't feel like I'm judging you. I was the king of this. I was sly though. I wouldn't go brag about it to everybody. Instead, I would casually mention it to someone I knew would brag about it for me. That way, everybody knew how awesome I was, and, as a bonus, I got a gold star for modesty too. That's an empty life.

When you climb to the top of life's mountains, take a second to enjoy the view before being compelled to pull out your phone for a picture to show everyone else. It's your life. Live it.

<u>Lesson 11: laughter is real (and it can be there when we need it most).</u>

[22] A joyful heart is good medicine, but a crushed spirit dries up the bones.
- Proverbs 17:22

Be kind to unkind people. They need it the most.
- Ashleigh Brilliant, author and cartoonist

Some people are always finding fault with Nature for putting thorns on roses; I always thank her for having put roses on thorns.
- Alphonse Karr, French novelist

My mom has always said Dad has given her the gift of laughter in her life. Most of my dad's jokes are terrible. His jokes make other dad jokes cringe. It's fine though. Having terrible jokes is a rite of passage that comes with dadhood. I too honor this timeless tradition. His bad jokes aside, my dad is literally always jolly and in a good mood. His laughter and love of life is infectious. His cheer has the ability to make difficult times a little easier.

Once Dad took George to buy throwing stars because George loved martial arts. George had to use a wheelchair because he couldn't walk without gasping for breath. A self-righteous grump was passing by as they were getting to the car and assumed they were just playing around with the wheelchair. He snarkily asked, "What's the matter with him?" Dad had his back turned, opening the car door on the passenger side while George sat in the wheelchair waiting. Without turning around, Dad said, "He has a chronic heart disorder." Dad opened the door, and George stood up to get in. The old man then said, "Ah, there's nothing really the matter with him." My first reaction honestly would've been to pummel the guy. At the very least, I would've indignantly berated him in defense of George. Dad, however, threw his hands up without a pause and started shouting, "It's a miracle! It's a miracle!" The man started cursing and walked on into the store. Dad started laughing and George began to crack up too.

George was twelve years old when this happened and was in a period where he was extremely sick. Even getting cleaned up and riding in a car was more than he could manage some days. He would become overexerted and have horrible migraines. My parents would have to turn around and take him home before they even reached town. He hated the wheelchair because people would stare at him, but Dad turned this situation into something George could laugh about. If he would've gotten angry or confrontational with the man, Bubby would have become even more self-conscious. It could've left him not wanting to get out in public at all with his wheelchair which would've essentially meant he was secluded to his home.

Another time, my family had taken me and my high school girlfriend to the movies. We were a typical high school couple that broke up repeatedly only to get back together again. I was a turd and was very flirtatious with one particular girl during all of our "off sessions". Naturally, the family of the girl I had been flirting with was not a fan of me once I got back with my original girlfriend. Anyway, we were walking to our car after the movie and this other girl was walking in with some of her family. A grown man who was with them used his hand to make an "L" on his forehead and screamed, "Loser!" When you get past the absurdity of a grown man behaving like a twelve-year-old, a natural reaction as a father might have been to lash out at the man. My dad had never even heard of this girl or anyone in her family. He had no idea who these people were or why this man called me a loser. Since Dad didn't hang out with many ten-year old girls, I am fairly certain he had never even seen the dreadful "L" hand and loser taunt. Nonetheless, without skipping a beat, my dad used his hands to make a "W" on his forehead and launched back, "Whatever!" Once more, the guy didn't know how to react to my dad's ridiculousness, so he just walked on in.

Everyone besides Dad had been stunned so we were silent until we got into the car. Once inside, Dad casually asks, "Who were those people?" We all broke out laughing that the initial, knee-jerk reaction of my dad, who was in his late 30's at the time, was to release his inner teenager with the appropriate counter-burn. You can't fake that level of absurd cheer and positivity. In a moment where some random guy is childishly attacking his son, he still used laughter to diffuse the situation.

My dad has brought the gift of laughter to all of our lives. His legacy won't be that he was full of laughter and joy in the good times; it will be that this remained his natural disposition in the bad times too. He is able to appreciate life and laugh when times are tough. In George's essay *The Intervention of Angels,* he talked about the lowest moment of his life, coming out from his transplant only to realize that his struggles were not over as he had hoped for. Dad's joking with the nurse that he also needed his hair washed helped him have a more positive outlook and to keep pushing forward. Dad taught me that following Christ isn't a burdensome, somber life consumed by rigid rule following and judgment of others who fail to live up to our standards. When somebody truly appreciates Christ's gift of this life and the one to come, what else is left to do other than laugh?

Laughter Action Challenge

Most of this book deals with serious issues. Don't allow yourself to become so consumed with working toward a better life that you lose sight of why you're doing all the work in the first place. Life is a gift. Cherish it.

- As your natural disposition, do you find joy and laughter in life? Explain with specific examples.

- Describe a time when your laughter helped someone else through a tough situation (or someone else's laughter helped you through a tough situation).

Lifestyle change:

Often, we are faced with times where reacting in anger would be justified, but our frustrations will only further complicate an already tough situation. The next time you face a difficult circumstance, try to resist the urge to react negatively and instead respond in a light-hearted nature. This won't happen magically. It will stem from the fact that your daily life is rooted in love and laughter. For you to succeed in this lifestyle change, you have to approach every aggravating moment, even the seemingly small ones, with intentionality to remain the best version of yourself even in the midst of frustration.

Lesson 12: God's plan is real (and it's not based on what you can do).

³ Now Moses was a very humble man, more humble than anyone else on the face of the earth.

- Numbers 12:3

¹⁰ Moses said to the Lord, "Pardon your servant, Lord. I have never been eloquent, neither in the past nor since you have spoken to your servant. I am slow of speech and tongue."

- Exodus 4:10

² Now there was no water for the community, and the people gathered in opposition to Moses and Aaron. ³They quarreled with Moses and said, "If only we had died when our brothers fell dead before the Lord! ⁴Why did you bring the Lord's community into this wilderness, that we and our livestock should die here? ⁵ Why did you bring us up out of Egypt to this terrible place? It has no grain or figs, grapevines or pomegranates. And there is no water to drink!" ⁶ Moses and Aaron went from the assembly to the entrance to the tent of meeting and fell facedown, and the glory of the Lord appeared to them. ⁷ The Lord said to Moses, ⁸ "Take the staff, and you and your brother Aaron gather the assembly together. Speak to that rock before their eyes and it will pour out its water. You will bring water out of the rock for the community so they and their livestock can drink." ⁹ So Moses took the staff from the Lord's presence, just as he commanded him. ¹⁰ He and Aaron gathered the assembly together in front of the rock and Moses said to them, "Listen, you rebels, must we bring you water out of this rock?" ¹¹ Then Moses raised his arm and struck the rock twice with his staff. Water gushed out, and the community and their livestock drank. ¹² But the Lord said to Moses and Aaron, "Because you did not trust in me enough to honor me as holy in the sight of the Israelites, you will not bring this community into the land I give them."

- Numbers 20:2-12

Where You go, I'll go
Where You stay, I'll stay
When You move, I'll move
I will follow
               - "I will follow" by Chris Tomlin

Long ago, God had assured Abraham that his descendants would flourish in a promised land, but the Israelites had been captive slaves in Egypt for hundreds of years. The verses for this lesson depict Moses trying to convince God he isn't the right person to lead the Israelites out of Egypt. There were over six-hundred thousand Israelite men, and biblical scholars estimate there were more than two million women and children. Moses is telling God he is slow of speech and tongue. He has a stuttering problem, and he believes that will prohibit him from inspiring the masses to follow him.

Moses was the most humble man on Earth. We often look at humility as an undesirable trait in a leader, but this is a flawed perception of leadership. Moses' humility didn't only make him aware of his own limitations and his need for God; it taught him that what he could do on his own didn't matter. Instead, it was about what the Father could do through him. God sent Moses' older brother, Aaron, to help him speak and deliver His message.

Moses led God's chosen people through unbelievable trials and obstacles. His faith remained when Pharaoh sent armies to chase down the Israelites and trapped them at the edge of the Red Sea. When there was no way forward, Moses lifted his staff and God parted the waters. When the Israelites faced dehydration and starvation in the desert, his reliance on God endured even though all others lost faith. He stayed true when he received The Ten Commandments while the rest turned toward false idols. It would have been natural to become proud of his faith and works. I mean, the guy literally split a sea in half. Not a lot of people can put that on their resume. Still, Moses remained humble in spirit.

I was thinking the other day that it was unfair that God did not allow Moses into the promised land of Canaan. He showed a brief moment of doubt in God and pride in himself.

After enduring the constant complaints and doubts of the Israelites for forty years, he made a single mistake by breaking faith with God during the last year of their journey. As the people cried out in despair for water, he brought water from a rock by tapping it with his staff. The Bible doesn't directly state why his actions were a sin. It could've been because he did not give credit to God when he drew out the water or that he did it in a different way than God had commanded.

Moses was on the precipice of fulfilling one of the greatest achievements in the history of man. He had overseen the fulfillment of God's promise to Abraham and delivered his people, but now he would be denied entry at the door. He did more to get God's people there than anyone, so in my mind he deserves the greatest reward. His faith and work had earned him the honor of finishing out this race. He had every right to be indignant that God would punish him so severely for a single mistake. After all, he had parted the Red Sea, talked directly to God himself, remained the most faithful of all of God's chosen people, and transcribed the backbone of Jewish law—The Ten Commandments. If anyone deserved recognition and special favor from God, it was Moses. After reflection, I realized there are two faults with this reasoning that impact my life:

1) We don't deserve anything. I lived my life trying to be perfect to earn the gifts I was given. I worked for others, and I worked for God to prove my worth. My actions are meaningless unless I am doing God's will for God's purpose. Moses served God simply because he was a servant of God. Servants don't expect rewards. I get so caught up in the work I can do for God sometimes that I forget that my purpose is solely to love. Love whoever God sends my way in whatever means I can.

2) Why does it really matter if he made it to the promised land? I put too much emphasis on the rewards I receive on Earth. If Moses spent a day or a hundred years there, that is nothing compared to an eternity in Heaven. Moses wasn't working toward a temporary reward here. I spent so much of my life working for

recognition. I wanted to be the best teacher in the entire world. That seems ludicrous to say, but it is what I wanted. It's what I worked for. Not only did I want to be the best teacher, but I wanted everyone else to recognize me as the greatest teacher on the planet. Moses was not concerned with rewards or acclaim. He was concerned with doing God's will.

Moses didn't plead to God that this punishment was unfair. He didn't boast of all the times he had maintained his faith while others had fallen away. Instead, he asked God to appoint a worthy new leader so the Israelites would not become lost. He led the people of Israel through serving them and serving God even when it no longer offered any possibility of personal reward on Earth. Moses started the journey as a humble man who did not believe himself worthy of this great task God had set before him. After overcoming the entire Egyptian army single-handedly at the Red Sea and speaking directly to God himself at the burning bush, Moses still ended the journey as the same humble man. He was God's servant through the good times and the bad, always putting the needs of others above his own.

Like Moses, my dad is humble and thought his personal shortcomings would prevent him from leading God's people. In the early months of 1991, God was leading Dad to become a minister. My dad struggled to read and was afraid to follow this calling because the words of any real preacher are based on scripture. If he struggled to read the passages aloud as he preached, he assumed this would hinder God's message and ultimately prevent him from fulfilling God's purpose for him. Also like Moses, Dad was concentrating on his abilities instead of accepting that we can do all things through Christ. If we work earnestly to fulfill God's purpose, He will make a way.

One day, as Dad was pouring his heart out at the altar praying for George, he told God that he wanted to follow Him, but he simply could not preach on his own. He had the desire but felt his lack of education was too much to overcome. He told God that if it was His will, He would have to send him help. My dad looked up, and my mom was standing in front of him. God told him, "I have already given you your help." On June 23rd,

1991 (the six-year anniversary of rededicating his life to God) my dad accepted the call to ministry.

My mom helped him study and practice reading for all of his sermons. He would ask her how to pronounce certain words and the meaning of others. She went to every service he preached. God helped my dad grow in confidence and knowledge as the years rolled on so he did not have to rely on Mom so much during his studies. He became the Pastor at Morgan Branch Pentecostal on June 30th, 1996 when he was thirty-two years old. Twenty-four years later, he still serves in the same role.

In the end, God's plan for my dad was fulfilled not in spite of his struggles to read but because of them. He had to study more intently with deep concentration on each word. It made him slow down enough to truly be with scripture. He doesn't just read the Bible like it is a textbook to be mastered and controlled, but rather as a love letter from God with His words speaking directly into his life. He has a deeper understanding of the Bible than anyone I have ever met. When he preaches, he delivers the Word in a way that makes it seem so simple and clear. He has taken his love for God and shared it from behind the pulpit for almost thirty years now. He doesn't speak as a scholar, proudly citing all the verses he has memorized and the nuances that only he can understand. He speaks as God's child to the rest of God's children.

Today, countless lives have been changed because Dad decided to follow God's plan even though he was afraid. Like Moses, Dad has led God's people with no expectation of personal gain. He has put the needs of his church above his own at every opportunity. And today, my dad is still that same humble man. All the glory of all of the great deeds he's ever done, he freely gives to God. He knows it isn't his strength but God's that allows for the miracles seen every day in the changing lives of those who once were lost but now are found.

I've always wondered, how could a single man such as Moses lead such a big crowd? I mean, he couldn't text out information or post updates on social media. There were over two million people following the lead of this one man. The majority of them couldn't have had much interaction with him.

Today, I realized the answer to that question. It was pastor appreciation day at my dad's church. Person after person spoke about how my dad had impacted them. It didn't matter if it was our family or someone who hadn't known him very long, the same key words kept popping up again and again. Love. Joy. Laughter. Father figure. And, of course, goofball. It hit me that everyone I know follows my dad because they trust where he's leading them. They know without a shadow of a doubt he loves them and spends his life trying to make their lives better. That's how Moses led that multitude. When troubles came and they would struggle, they knew following Moses would lead them back where they needed to be. The same is true with Dad. Dad may have social media available while Moses didn't, but they use it about the same amount. Dad doesn't need a method to reach a multitude. He makes an instantaneous connection with everyone he meets, and the same had to be true for Moses. Every person he interacts with knows he loves them from the second they meet with him.

Humility is what allows for that authentic care. The belief that everyone matters. He's unique. He doesn't just say he cares; he actually cares. He doesn't just fake a smile because it is polite; he really smiles. And when he says he's going to pray for you, he really prays. My dad and Moses both followed the example Christ set for us all. As Mark 10:43-45 says, Christ came not to be served but to serve. To effectively lead others means to be a servant to all. This self-sacrifice is only possible through humility and the love for others that arises from it.

God has a different plan for us all. He planned for Moses to lead the greatest revolution in human history. He planned for my dad to lead everyone in his life. I don't know what He has planned for you specifically, but all of His plans have one unifying theme: love. He plans for you to love every day and in every way possible. Whatever path He's leading you down, be confident enough to follow. You don't have to have everything it takes to complete the task, all you have to have is love. He'll take care of the rest. We don't just need to give our ten percent tithe. We don't just show up on Sunday in our fancy clothes. For God to work through us, we need to give all of ourselves.

Everything we are and everything we will ever be. Give yourself and have faith that God will use you to fulfill His purpose.

God's Plan Action Challenge
- Has there been a calling or action that you have felt compelled to do? Describe it below.

Does this task seem impossible or beyond your abilities? Often, the things we aren't good at seem to be the tasks God calls us to do. It may seem counterintuitive at first, but it makes a lot of sense. God doesn't want us to rely on ourselves. Ultimately, that would end in failure. We are to believe in God and rely on Him. Live out God's plan for your life. If you choose not to fulfill it, no one else can.
- What is one action you can take today to step out in faith on the path that God has laid out for you to walk? All you have to do is take the first step, then God will send you the help you need.

Lifestyle change:

It is so easy to become fixated on what we can accomplish in our own strength. It's great that you give food to the poor. Still, God let manna fall from the sky to feed the Israelites during their exodus from Egypt. It is amazing if you have the confidence to share your story in public to glorify God, but God delivered the Ten Commandments to Moses from a burning bush. The one and only thing we truly have to give the world is love. Free will love. It is the only thing God cannot raise a rock up to do in our place. If He forced us to love, then it is no longer our choice and thus is no longer love. A life of love is filled with laughter. Even when we question the path we're on and doubt ourselves, we can have faith God will lead us through. In this confidence, we have laughter at all times because we know we've already won. Today, I want you to write down an issue you have been struggling with and look at it from a different viewpoint. Instead of looking at it with fear and doubt, accept that you can and will accomplish this goal. Instead of focusing on the finish line, enjoy the steps you'll take to get there, and get started with that first step (or next step) today.

Lesson 13: your calling is real (and they may not fit into everyone else's idea of success).

[11] *"For I know the plans I have for you," declares the Lord, "plans to prosper you and not to harm you, plans to give you hope and a future."*
- Jeremiah 29:11

"Don't ask what the world needs. Ask what makes you come alive and go do it. Because what the world needs is people that have come alive."
- Howard Thurman, African-American author, religious leader, and civil-rights activist.

[3] *I tell you the truth, unless you change and become like little children, you will never enter the kingdom of Heaven. Therefore, whoever humbles himself like this little child is the greatest in the Kingdom of Heaven.*
- Matthew 18:3

If he was to become himself, he must find a way to assemble the parts of his dream into one whole.
- George Elliot, pen name of Victorian novelist Marian Evans

Your vision will become clear only when you look into your own heart. Who looks outside, dreams; who looks inside, awakes.
- Carl Jung

It is not the critic who counts; not the man who points out how the strong man stumbles, or where the doer of deeds could have done them better. The credit belongs to the man who is actually in the arena, whose face is marred by dust and sweat and blood; who strives valiantly; who errs, who comes short again and again; who spends himself in a worthy cause; who at the best knows in the end the triumph of high achievement, and who at the worst, if he fails, at least fails while daring greatly, so that his place shall never be with those cold and timid souls who neither know victory or defeat.
- "Citizenship in A Republic" by Theodore Roosevelt

My parents were seventeen when they started dating. Dad would go pick Mom up in his mother's car immediately after work, showing up without even taking the time to wash off the grease and sweat. His two older brothers went home when they finished hauling their loads for the day, but as the mechanic Dad had to stay and service the trucks. They had one car as a family. For him to be able to use it, he couldn't let his brothers finish getting cleaned up first. He'd go pick my mom up filthy and drive back to his house for a shower. About the only other place he went was church.

When my parents got married, Dad carried everything he owned in a bag: one work uniform that had to be washed every night, one pair of pants, and two shirts my mom had bought him for his birthday in April three months before. They started their marriage with almost nothing. They worked and saved to provide the life they wanted for Alan and me. I didn't realize we were poor when I was growing up. We never made it to the level of starring on MTV Cribs (is that still a show?), but as I grew older we had a nice, stable home that my mom kept immaculately clean. Even so, in my early years, we had very little. I slept in my crib wearing my beanie (or as we call it in Kentucky—a boggin) because we didn't have heat. I think the breaking point in moving from our first house came when they found a snake under my crib that had crawled into the house through holes in the underpinning.

My dad didn't choose to work nearly every waking hour because he wanted to. He did it because he didn't have any other options as a man without a high school diploma. My dad is the greatest man I have ever known, and I saw how a decision made when he was eighteen years old dictated the rest of his life. He was another product of growing up poor in Appalachia without value being placed on education. His choices were basically to mine coal or haul it. He chose the latter.

I've wondered often how my dad's life would've turned out had he had someone pushing him in school. He could've honed his skills in mathematics to become an engineer. Perhaps he would've found an opportunity in trade school where he could have applied his mechanical knowledge. He just needed somebody to tell him that, as an intelligent person with the strongest work ethic I have ever seen, his options were limitless. Ultimately, that person wasn't in his life. Instead, he chose to quit school. What he didn't realize at the time is that he wasn't just deciding to quit school, but he was choosing everything that came with that decision. He was choosing to set an alarm for 1:30 a.m. for the next thirty years. He was choosing to be so exhausted that he would fall asleep any time he sat in a chair for more than five minutes. He was choosing to have to eat fast food in his truck because stopping to eat meant losing time and money. He was choosing a path that would make him more susceptible to the disease of diabetes that would kill his dad and had killed his grandma. He was choosing a life that would break his body down well before his time.

The first time I remember someone asking me what I wanted to be when I grew up is when I was eight years old in my third grade class. I replied without hesitation that I wanted to be a teacher. I knew then that being a teacher was my professional purpose. Not only teaching, but teaching in Appalachia. I have seen what a lack of education can do to a life. My dad will die a younger man because of how much he loved my family and me. He pushed his body past its limits, but things didn't have to be that way. I decided that I would be that person in the lives of Appalachian kids to push them to be more than they thought they could be. The problems are glaringly clear for all to see. Economic ruin leaves families stuck in a cycle of drug abuse and welfare. The families that manage to avoid drugs often still have little hope of escaping poverty. I would help kids to realize there were more options than what they had seen in their lives. The alternative to repeating the cycle for most was to finish high school, get the first job that could put food on the table, and commit to grinding away their lives to provide for their families. I would make them understand that just because they were willing to work themselves to death didn't mean they should. I would stop people from making the decision my dad made.

Sadly, me being set on becoming a teacher was not a popular decision. Most family members told me I was wasting my intelligence. A lot of my teachers had become disenfranchised with the politics of education and told me it was not worth the frustration. Everyone agreed the pay was terrible.

My four best friends from high school are still four of my best friends today. One became a doctor. Another is a dentist. One is a lawyer. The last is a pharmacist. All pursued noble professions that paid a lot more money than a teacher. Pretty much everyone told me to pick one of those jobs, or really any other job. Just don't teach. My parents supported my decision because they support me in everything.

My mom had been the salutatorian of her graduating class, but her parents had really never even broached college as a possibility. She could have become anything she dreamed to be, but she was never pushed to dream. She began working as a bank teller right out of high school. She is now a manager for a prominent banking company. Still, I'm not sure this was ever really her professional calling. Sure, she has succeeded, but she would have succeeded at anything she pursued. My mom reads more than any person I've ever met. She reads at least two or three books a week. She is on her seventh Kindle because her non-stop reading keeps burning the lights out of them. I gathered a large group of beta-readers to give me feedback for this book. Due to my obsession with time management, I had them reading the book behind my editor as he reviewed. I granted everyone access and told them to wait to move on to Dad's section while my editor finished up. Well, she's my mom so I can't tell her what to do. Within three days, she had not only finished this entire book, but she had also read the outlines for the entire book series (remember, this series was originally developed as a single book). What if someone had pushed her toward this passion? Maybe it would be her writing books instead of me. She's wonderfully artistic. She could have pursued that gift. The specific career doesn't really matter. It's not a career question, but a purpose one. As the introductory quote in this lesson says, the world needs people who have come alive. She supported me in my pursuit of education because she understood its value. More than that, she understood that teaching would never be about the content for me. It was about the person.

My dad did what he always did, he told me he was proud of me. He knew that I had inherited his servant heart, but I don't think he ever knew the influence his life had on my decision. I wanted to help the Appalachian youth become who they could be. Our people are often mocked for our accents or labeled with demeaning stereotypes. I know the truth of the strength of these people. Many of them climb out of nothing to become successful with little to no support. I saw the genuine care that people had for one another, and I wanted to help push them to extend this care to themselves and their prospective careers. I don't believe there are too many men like my dad out there in the world, but I know there are many in our region that are of a similar mold. I wanted to help these people grow to share their brilliance with the people of Appalachia and the world.

Outside of my parents, I remember my uncle Dave telling me he thought I'd be a great teacher and telling me to follow my dream. Besides that, I can't recall anyone else glowing with support for the idea. It didn't matter though. I really didn't need anyone to support my decision. I knew what I was meant to do when I was eight years old, and I know it still today. My purpose was to empower kids. My parents settled for careers because they didn't know other options were available to them. Poverty smothers the lives of so many in Appalachia. Often, avoiding certain careers isn't even a conscious choice for students in poverty. They don't dare dream big because they believe big dreams do not exist for them. I wanted to let them know their lives were their own. Limitless possibilities were available to them just as much as they were any other kid in America. I got the chance to push kids to strive to not only be great students but to also be great people. I was able to impact so many lives and was blessed by them making a difference in mine. I got the opportunity to love going to work every day for eleven years. Not a lot of people get to say that.

Obviously our career choice isn't the only pathway to fulfilling our purpose. My parents have more than fulfilled God's calling for their life in different avenues. They have found their passion, love, and fulfillment in their church and family. We are called to be a light on a hill. That doesn't just mean while we're at work or home but in every second of our lives. My parents have shown that light for me and everyone who has been blessed to know them. I am merely trying to say that all of life is a gift—home, work, and everywhere in between. Ideally, we should find fulfillment in all parts of life. God has given each of us specific gifts and desires. Use those gifts to the best of your ability to become who he has called you to become in all facets of life.

Your Calling Action Challenge
- If you feel like you are currently fulfilling your calling, I want you to detail below how you are actually serving the people you thought you would serve.

- If you feel like you never made it to your professional calling, how can you still serve the people you feel called to serve in the life you have now? My dad never felt a deep gratification from hauling coal, but he found a way to serve as a pastor. Where in your life could you give back to the people you feel called to serve using your unique gifts?

Lifestyle change:
      Instead of looking back on your childhood dreams with judgment and harshness, today I want you to examine them in a light-hearted way. Maybe your dream of being in the Chicago Symphony Orchestra was a little far-fetched, but that doesn't mean you should've laid down your instrument altogether. Laugh at the unabashed confidence of childhood and allow yourself to see the underlying desire behind the sometimes outlandish goals. Then, laugh most heartily at how we as adults lose all of this confidence and instead become too afraid to risk anything at all for our goals. Laugh at that person you will no longer be. Find some of that childhood confidence that knows

you can do anything you put your mind to.

You don't have to be like me, and I don't have to be like you. Some of you are more introverted and shy, so the thought of spewing out words of love makes you feel like you need to spew something else as well. How many people you love isn't what matters. Rather, it's how much you love those you are given the opportunity to. Our calling is to love faithfully the people God has given us to love, whether it be three or three thousand. If we take a look back at our childhoods, we can see clues to the way God has chosen for us to love. Today, pick back up something that makes your life more enjoyable but you have laid down through the years due to the restraints and stress that come with being an adult. Use this gift to add love and joy to someone's life. The things we are naturally drawn to can allow us to express our love to the world even without saying it.

Lesson 14: forgiveness is real (and love cannot be earned or lost).

32 Be kind and compassionate to one another, forgiving each other, just as in Christ God forgave you.
- Ephesians 4:32

8 But God demonstrates his own love for us in this: While we were still sinners, Christ died for us.
- Romans 5:8

34 But Jesus was saying, "Father, forgive them; for they do not know what they are doing."
- Luke 23:34

Our children need to know that we're there to help them pick up the pieces of their shattered dreams, to tell them that they're okay, to help them see that failure isn't final, and that when they take their next steps, they will not be alone.
- Uncommon by Tony Dungy

    When I was twenty-three, I had been dating my girlfriend at the time for about nine months. We were at a bar for a New Year's celebration. Of course, nothing was a celebration when I was drinking, so I ended up making a fool of myself. We were arguing over something I can't even remember, and she left the bar. Later on that night, I tried to call her to start the fight back again. Another man answered the phone. I started belligerently yelling at this guy who was with my girlfriend at three in the morning. I don't remember anything I said specifically, only that I was incoherently threatening him.

    The next morning, I get a call from my brother asking me if I'm okay. He says my parents are worried about me and that my dad called him at around 3:00 a.m. distraught. Dad was worried about me and wanted to drive up to Lexington to help me. My brother wouldn't tell him where I was. Alan called one of my friends to make sure I was okay, and then he called Dad back to let him know I was alright. It turns out that guy I was cursing in the middle of the night was my dad, the man I've looked up to my whole life. My ex-girlfriend's name was Hope, but I had called "Home".

I was devastated to have shown this pathetic side of myself to my dad. I wanted him to believe I was a good son and a good person. I had been given every opportunity to be someone who could help change the world for the good. My dad and George are two of the greatest men to ever walk the Earth, but their sphere of influence was so relatively small. In a funeral home full of people paying their respects to George, a lot of them barely knew him. I can't count the number of people who have told me that the genuine love he showed them changed their lives even though they only met him a couple times. George was restricted by his health to a point that many people never received the blessing of meeting him. Probably the place he visited most often outside of a sixty-mile radius of our hometown was the hospital. Even then, the nurses and doctors would tell us of how inspiring he was and that they had never seen a patient show such optimism and strength. My dad spent seventy hours a week behind the wheel of a coal truck. The most giving person I've ever known gave so much of himself to his family that he had little time left over to be out in the world to shine his light for them. I had been given the gift of knowing these men and learning from them. I was supposed to be the person who took their lessons out to the world. I was supposed to make the world better not because of who I am but because of who they were. I had spent my life trying to be for the world who they were for me. But I had just shown my dad I wasn't that person. I was a pathetic, angry drunk throwing his life away and giving nothing to the world.

Hope justifiably broke up with me for acting the way I had. I stayed in my apartment for three days hiding in shame. I denied every call, ignored every text. I always felt miserable and guilt-ridden after one of my drunken tornadoes of destruction but behaving like that toward my father was unforgivable. I don't really know what my plan was. I had been in my apartment for three days in isolation. I didn't have any idea of when I would have the courage to face the world again. As I wallowed in self-pity and disgust, I heard a knock at my door. When I opened it, there stood Dad. He had driven two hours to my apartment without calling because he knew I would leave. I just dropped my head in humiliation and stood there silently. He put his arms around me and said words I will never forget. "Son, you could never do anything to make me stop loving you." That moment more than any other in my life showed me what love really is.

Too many people are confused with the purpose of forgiveness, thinking "I'm not forgiving them until they apologize." Forgiveness is not for the other person. Jesus shows us that forgiveness does not require the person being sorry. He hung on the cross and looked out on the people who spit on Him, mocked Him, and who were murdering Him slowly in the most horrendous way. As he endured the most painful moment in human history, he prayed "Father, forgive them for they know not what they do." My dad didn't forgive me because I asked him to or because I deserved it. He forgave me because he loved me. He forgave me because he had first been forgiven. Romans 5:8 says Jesus died for us while we were still sinners. He gave his life without us asking. He forgave without us saying we're sorry. Love cannot be earned. And the amazing thing is that if love cannot be earned, then it cannot be lost either. Love just is.

Forgiveness Action Challenge

Love those who don't deserve to be loved. Forgiveness is not forgetting about it, acting like it didn't happen, ignoring it, etc. Forgiveness is relinquishing the right or desire to get even. It's taking back your freedom.

- Have you been holding back forgiveness, harboring resentment against someone or some action? I want you to list all the benefits your refusal to forgive has given you. In other words, how has holding on to this grudge helped you?

Lifestyle Change:

Look back up at your list of benefits. I'm guessing it's an empty space. Hatred hurts the container. It's like drinking poison and waiting for the other person to get sick. As long as you harbor hate, you're a prisoner to that person and the deed that caused you pain. Part of your life is stuck in that moment. You may be justified by your resentment, but life isn't about justice. If you hold onto grudges against those who've wronged you, then that resentment will smother out the rest of your life. It will consume you. Holding on to the wrongs that others have done to us robs our life of joy and laughter.

Maybe you are ready to forgive today, but maybe the pain is too much and the scar too deep right now. Today, take a step, no matter how small, toward forgiveness This forgiveness isn't for them, it's for you. Take your life back. Start moving toward leaving your pain in the past and give yourself the freedom to laugh again.

Part 4: Meet my daughter and my angel, Georgia Reid, who taught me...

My chunk using her belly button to save her sucker for later

Georgia and my nephew Sebastian (Bash)

Me and my baby

Her general feelings about my shenanigans

My two girls, Georgia and Sarah

Daddy/Daughter dance

My angel

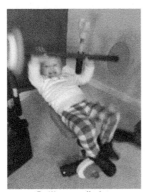

Getting swolled up

Looking way too old

She would kill me if I didn't include her cat, Callie

They're both convinced this photoshopped butterfly actually landed on her hand

Pinnacles Hiking Trail – Berea, KY (this is the hike when she was complaining about her legs being tired)

Georgia never got to meet George. I simply asked her, "Who was George to me?"
George in Georgia's words:

- *He is your best friend*
- *He is your hero*
- *He is why my name is Georgia.*

Lifestyle change: Realize that your life is bigger than you. Your actions extend beyond yourself. When you love, your love multiplies itself through others. When you fail to do so, this lack of love also compounds itself. For each action challenge in this part, realize you're not just doing it for yourself. Your willingness to take this action means the ones you love are much more likely to do the same.

Lesson 15: purpose is real (and you never know when the example you set will pay off).

> *21 What benefit did you reap at that time from the things you are now ashamed of? Those things result in death!*
> *- Romans 6:21*

> *5 The purposes of a person's heart are deep waters, but one who has insight draws them out.*
> *- Proverbs 20:5*

> *23 The steps of a man are established by the Lord, when he delights in His way; 24 though he fall, he shall not be cast headlong, for the Lord upholds his hand.*
> *- Psalms 37:23-24*

> *He who has a why to live can endure almost any how.*
> *- Friedrich Nietzsche*

> *Being your daddy comes natural*
> *The roses just know how to grow*
> *- "Letting You Go" by Jason Isbell*

I'm going to watch you shine. I'm going to watch you grow.
I'm going to paint a sign so you'll always know,
as long as one and one is two
there could never be a father love his daughter more than I love
you.
- "Fathers and Daughters" by Paul Simon

My mom helped me make this, and it hangs in Georgia's room. I sang this song to her every night when she was little. She hates it now and always makes me skip it when it comes on her playlist. Oh well. It's still our song.

From George's death in 2004 to January of 2014, I buried my shame, guilt, and bitterness deep inside. On January 6, 2014, I was watching Jameis Winston lead the Florida State Seminoles to a national championship, and Hope came in to deliver the news that she was pregnant. In my shock and denial, I drove directly to the store to buy two more pregnancy tests. Sure enough, I was going to be a daddy.

I've heard it said the mother feels her maternal bond well before the man can earnestly experience a fatherly connection to their child. This generalization was not descriptive of my experience. As soon as I knew Georgia existed, I felt my love for her. As soon as the third pregnancy test was positive (a scientist needs replicable data to prove validity), she was Georgia in my heart.

I remember talking with someone in high school about what we would name our kids. They told me several girl names they liked and a couple boy names. When it was my turn, I simply said, "Georgia." When they asked what my other names were, I said, "There aren't any." When they asked, "What if it is a boy?" I simply replied, "She won't be." I knew that I would name my child after George. I also knew he hated the name George, so I couldn't name a boy that. I was meant to be a dad, and I was meant to honor him. She was always Georgia.

Teaching was my calling, but there were times I wasn't a teacher. I poured my heart into the profession, but I also lived much of my life separate from this role. I was born to be Georgia Lynn Reid's Daddy. That is the purpose of my life. It has impacted every breath I have taken and every decision I have made since that moment on January 6, 2014. Everything I do, I do as her Daddy.

For the decade prior, I had needed help in the most desperate way. My life had slipped through my fingers as I tried to hold onto who I had been. Although my longing for support was deep, my pride was more important to me than my well-being. I couldn't admit my pain for fear of being perceived as weak. I couldn't reveal my shame due to my cowardice and dread of being held accountable. I had been able to fight through just enough to have my life at least appear to be okay. That was enough for me. I had held onto my pride in spite of the fact that it had made me let go of any hope of real peace or joy. I loved my pride more than I loved myself or anything else in the world. Georgia changed that. She was the only thing I loved more than my pride. She made me care enough to truly give life another try.

The next day, on January 7, 2014, I bought my first self-help book. I began the arduous process of peeling back all the layers of self-reliance, fictitious strength, and imitation joy I had built up to protect myself. I began to at least try to rediscover my real self. I began the journey to try to save that boy who had never been able to leave the side of a hospital bed on July 14th of 2004.

Purpose Action Challenge

I heard Dean Hood, the former head football coach at Eastern Kentucky University, give a speech at a football conference once. Unlike most coaches who focused on the X's and O's of football, he talked about the importance of teaching our players how to be good men. He said once a year he would lead the team through a character day, highlighting the attributes they would need to truly be successful in life. This inspired me to create my own character day in my classroom that I continued for the next nine years. It became the most important day of the year for me. Hopefully, it was the most important day for many of my students as well.

In his speech, he talked about what he called The Great Exchange: "Are you willing to trade what you want the most for what you want right now?" Many of life's failures occur because we give up our heart's deepest desires for momentary, fleeting gratification. Husbands or wives are willing to give up their families for an affair. Students are willing to give up their integrity to cheat on a test. Bosses are willing to betray their employees' trust for a little extra money in their pocket. Athletes are willing to give up their respect for the game for performance enhancing drugs.

- What is it you want the most? What is the single most important thing in your life? Instead of writing it here, I want you to write it on three separate Post-It Notes. If you don't have Post-It Notes, you can just write it on three small pieces of paper and put a piece of tape along the top.
- Now, I want you to think of the three things that most often tempt you to give up the thing you want most. Go place the Post-It Notes on those three things you sometimes choose in the moment instead of what you really want.
    - Example: You want to be healthy but struggle with overeating. Maybe you would write "health" on your Post-It Notes and then stick them on the refrigerator, microwave, and pantry.
    - Example 2: Maybe you want to love your wife

and be the father your child deserves, but you struggle to abstain from pornography. You could write "family" on your notes and place them on the laptop and beside the lock to your door. If you struggle with this temptation, your phone is a major threat. Take a picture of the third Post-It and make it your background.

Lifestyle change:

Character is not a switch you can turn on and off. I knew that. I could fake it in front of everyone else, but I knew eventually Georgia would see behind the mask. I knew she would see me when I didn't know she was looking, and she'd know the real me. I couldn't tell her that love and kindness matter and still live a life where those things didn't exist. I said the reason I felt an immediate connection to her was because I've always known her and who she would be. I hope that's true. I fear another reason is that I knew just how screwed up I was. I felt the immediate need to try to gather up the shambles of my life and throw together something that resembled a man who could be a father.

The next time you face the temptation of being less than you are, you will see that Post-It note. In that moment, you'll have to decide if you are willing to sacrifice what you want the most for what you want right now. Only you can make that choice. Accept that whatever choice you make, the ones you love are more likely to make that decision as well.

<u>Lesson 16: limiting beliefs are real (and your life can't truly move forward as long as they remain).</u>
It could be that we are driven by a need to perform and feel that we are worthwhile only when we are achieving and doing.
- Sacred Rhythms by Ruth Haley Barton

[27] *All things are possible with God.*
- Mark 10:27

Examine your beliefs and break free.
- Maria Erving

Even though I vowed to get better for Georgia, I was still determined to do it alone. I had to be tough enough to overcome this. It was imperative for my inner strength to be enough. My insistence on self-reliance meant I was starting a journey to recovery I was destined to never finish. Losing George was devastating, but that singular moment had not led to me destroying my entire life. It wasn't my failure to show him enough love. It wasn't the haunting knowledge that if I had shown him his beauty, worth, and importance, he wouldn't have believed the doctor's insinuation that he was a burden on others. What crippled my life was the mindset I developed because of these things. It was a suffocatingly assured belief that prevented me from authentic recovery: I am not enough. Resoundingly. Emphatically. Irreversibly. I was not enough so I am not enough. I am not enough so I will never be enough.

I had tried climbing this mountain of debilitating certainty my entire adult life, but I had never been able to reach the summit. Even though I believed my inadequacy was undeniable, I refused to just give up entirely. My refusal to accept the truth spurred my refusal to show weakness. I mistakenly believed any hint of vulnerability proved my frailty. My self-reliance was so ingrained I never considered reaching out for help. I was responsible for destroying my life, and I would be the one to rebuild it.

The compulsion to be strong originated from a righteous longing to honor George and Dad, but it resulted in an inability to share intimacy. Ultimately, I knew I was not strong. For me to maintain the image of who I wanted to be, I could never let anyone close enough to see the warts. People suffering from depression have a tendency to dwell on negative thoughts. We turn them over and over in our minds. It's a toxic practice called rumination. It's healthy to do this briefly after a negative experience to process and accept the situation, but for us this becomes a constant habit. Rumination is one of the core drivers to clinical depression. It amplifies the intensity of our negative mood and initiates our stress response. We get so lost inside our heads that it damages our relationships with others.

I failed George, and I allowed that to become the cornerstone in a house built of inauthenticity, regret, and shame. Before George's death, I had been legitimately strong, loving, and whole. I offered and accepted love freely. My clinging to self-reliance in every problem I faced after I lost George led to me becoming a shell of my former self. To the world, I was the same. Inside, I was hollow. There was nothing. My refusal to share my pain meant I alone became judge and executioner of my life. My limiting belief began as "I was too weak to show George my true feelings that night in Myrtle Beach." Over a decade of rumination, it morphed into "I am weak." The root of my shame was initially "I was not enough for George the one time he truly needed me." Ultimately, it penetrated deep into my psyche, becoming "I am not enough." What started as one mistake, one moment of weakness, became my whole life. Everything I worked toward and everything I avoided could be traced back to this limiting belief. I only pursued things that gave validity to the image I wanted to portray. Every slip up was validation of my feelings of being deficient and flawed. Even my successes fueled this fire because they were artificial. I believed they were simply a mirage distracting people from the black hole inside.

Georgia was born on September 3rd, 2014. In October of 2015, she had been inside of a church one or two times. Deep in my core, I believed I wasn't worthy of forgiveness and avoided Jesus because of this. I knew He would forgive me if only I asked; I just didn't feel like I had the right to do so. On a Sunday during this month, Georgia was in a church for her third time because we were attending my dad's Pastor Appreciation Day.

Without warning, they asked for me to come to the front to talk about what my dad meant to me. I hadn't had time to create an elaborate tale that I knew would be impactful for the congregation. I walked to the pulpit feeling something I hadn't felt since I was a child: nervousness. My whole life was planned and staged to the point that I was always in complete control of everything around me. I was never nervous because I was able to dictate the story and the image I portrayed.

When I opened my mouth to speak, nothing came out. I looked out and saw Georgia sitting in her Pop's (my dad's) lap. This was extremely rare because she is a Nana's (my mom's) girl. If she's not with me, she always gravitates toward Mom. Seeing her there in Dad's lap was jolting for me. In that moment, I knew she would never feel about me like I did about my dad. She would see behind my mask of self-control and goodness to the weakness lurking beneath. I could play the role of an honorable man that I had created for everyone else, but eventually she would see the truth. I knew that if I was going to be the man she deserved, I couldn't do it on my own. So when I opened my mouth again, something unusual for me came out: the truth. I told of the depths of my struggles with alcohol. I admitted my weakness and my need for Christ. I got down on my knees and asked Jesus to forgive me. And, of course, He did. He came into my life and gave me a new hope. That day was the first real glimmer of light I had in my life. I had always known in my heart I was not enough, but this was the first time I had admitted this to anyone else. In this admission, my reliance on Christ was my first step toward actually exposing this supposed truth as the blatant lie that it is.

Even still, I approached my Christianity like I did everything else in my life. I worked to earn God's grace. On days I read my bible, I felt worthy of His love. On days when I didn't, I felt ashamed and tried to hide myself from Him. When I would feel my depression start to overwhelm me, I would pray harder. I thought if I just had more faith, I would be okay. I read more self-help books to try to become a better man. I felt like my mental and emotional struggles could simply be forced into submission. And still, I worked all alone. I didn't tell my church family of my struggles. I showed up on Sundays, felt renewed in

Christ's love, and then forged on toward my week knowing my struggles would inevitably return. At first, even though I didn't realize it, my relationship with Christ was about me, not Him. My focus was on what I could do for Him. It was all about my work, my dedication, my strength. I failed to realize that all Christ asks from us is love. Love for Him. Love for others. And love for ourselves. Over the next four years, I worked incessantly to be what Georgia deserved even though I knew I was not. The immensity of that undertaking can be seen through the sheer volume of quotes, verses, and lyrics that begin each of these lessons. These are only a fraction of the evidence of my efforts. Through all my work, I still never succeeded. I didn't get better because in my heart I knew I never could.

Limiting Beliefs Action Challenge

Sometimes when we ruminate on thoughts so long, we allow them to become fact. When you live inside your head, it is easy to let facts become confused with your interpretation of those facts. Yes, I left George on that balcony without expressing my love. No, that does not mean he did not know how much I loved him. Yes, I had been struggling with depression for more than a third of my life. No, that did not mean I could not possibly recover. Yet, due to my refusal to communicate with anyone in any way, I wouldn't come to these realizations until four years after Georgia was born.

- For the next three minutes, think about all of your personal weaknesses and shortcomings. List them here.

- Look back at that list but read them as if they are describing someone other than yourself. How many of those weaknesses are facts, and how many are simply your interpretation of facts?
    - An example would be a fact like "I have acne" versus the opinion "I am ugly." You may feel your acne makes you ugly, but that is only your opinion. Everyone has acne at certain stages in their life. What you assume is so repulsive may be something that other people don't even notice.
    - Another example of a fact about you might be "I lie." An interpretation of that fact is "I am a liar." The former refers to specific instances where you have been false with someone. The latter suggests your total lack of honesty. Few people are honest without fail, and we are often

harsher critics of our own morality because we assume we are the only people making mistakes.

- Some of these interpretations of facts will be just plain false (i.e. I am ugly). Some of them may resonate with the truth. In these instances, shifting your mindset about how you perceive them is crucial. Replacing "I am a liar" with "I lie often" in your mind may seem meaningless, but it most definitely is not. This subtle shift brings the description back to a measurable fact. Fortunately, there are direct actions you can take to counteract a fact like this and eventually eliminate it.
  - Make a t-chart with facts on one side and opinions on the other. For every weakness you listed above that was a fact, make a tally mark in the fact section. For every weakness that was your interpretation of a fact, make a mark in the opinion section.

Lifestyle change:

You've taken the hardest step by choosing to try to improve yourself. Don't waste the next four years holding on to the pride or fear that prevents you from talking to someone like I did.

This is a tough one. This week, I would like for you to have a conversation with the person you trust the most in the world. In this conversation, I want you to open up about how you see yourself and your life in this moment. That means sharing what you believe to be good and what you believe to be bad. I know it's tough to say, "Hey, listen to all these things I hate about myself and the situation I'm in." Still, I assure you that when you begin to get these limiting beliefs out of your head and into the world, you will find many of them simply are not true. What you have assumed to be facts will be exposed as merely opinion. Then, without these false limitations in your life, you can finally become what you really are.

If you are not willing to do this for yourself, I understand. I avoided sharing my true feelings for over a decade. If you can't do it for yourself, do it for the person you love and are going to talk to. I assure you they too have limiting beliefs. We all do. Because you opened up, they will be much more likely to do the same. Sacrifice your comfort for them. Step out on that ledge of vulnerability and watch your loved one join you.

Lesson 17: thoughts are real (and the negative vortex can suck you in).

9 ...for the Lord searches every heart and understands every motive behind the thoughts. If you seek him, he will be found by you...

- 1 Chronicles 28:9

Worry does not empty tomorrow of its sorrow, it empties today of its strength.

- Corrie Ten Boom, Dutch Christian watchmaker and writer

You must learn a new way to think before you can master a new way to be.

- Marianne Williamson

Whatever you hold in your mind on a consistent basis is exactly what you will experience in your life.

- Tony Robbins

Mindfulness and meditation were immensely impactful for me to remove the blinders I had placed on my life. I had operated under the certainty that I was a failure for so long that I had ceased to even question it. My life was focused on non-stop productivity. Even when I was watching a movie with Georgia or playing with her, part of my mind was dedicated to planning for things I could accomplish once she went to sleep. My refusal to communicate with anyone else made my need for meditation even greater. During periods of mindfulness, I could at least begin to become aware of my cycle of negative thoughts and begin to try to capture them.

During one of my meditation sessions, I came across a practice called The Gratitude Countdown. Tamara Levitt, the meditation expert who operates the Calm app, explained this practice as something that pulled her out of her perpetually negative mindset. The Gratitude Countdown can be practiced alone or with a partner. Your partner (or you if you are practicing alone) will say aloud ten at which point you are to respond with something you are grateful for providing as much detail as possible. Immediately after your description, your partner will say nine and you follow with another item of thanks. This process continues until you finish with the number one. Then, if you are working with a partner, the roles switch.

Georgia and I sometimes practice this together. I came to notice nearly everything I was thankful for revolved around her. She was, and is, my world. Yet when I was playing with her, I would often be distracted by my thoughts and my phone. I would continually update my to-do list on Google Keep while we were together to the point where I spent as much time ignoring her as I did playing with her. The Gratitude Countdown helped me realize how I allotted my time to things that mattered much less than her. I had developed the toxic habit of fixating on all that was wrong with me rather than appreciating the countless gifts I had received in my life.

I began to keep my phone in the other room when we played to avoid the temptation of this distraction. Now, when we are beginning to play, if Georgia catches me looking at my phone, she automatically banishes it to another room. An unintended consequence of deliberately removing my phone was that my need to be productive became less urgent. My limiting beliefs that I was not enough and that I was a failure started to pierce my thoughts less frequently when I was with her. I also found that when I was fully present with her, I was more my true self than I had been since I was a teen. I began to control my thoughts instead of letting them control me. I was hers, and she was mine. And that's all that mattered.

It's easy to give our thoughts an elevated sense of importance. It's almost as if we consider our thoughts to be our "real self" and use them as proof to support our negative perceptions of ourselves. "You wouldn't think I was a good person if you knew all the stuff that went on in my head." Your thoughts are just another part of you. Your muscles move by your brain firing an electrochemical signal called an action potential. Your thoughts are generated by this same mechanism.

When we ruminate, our thoughts become real. They become who we perceive ourselves to be. In turn, our perceptions of ourselves then impact the way we behave. This self-fulfilling prophecy provides validation to our original thought, strengthening our assurance that we were right all along. In reality, our thoughts were the stimulus that caused both the emotion and the behavior.

I have always been aware of my tendency to spiral. I lived such a rigid life demanding perfection that every mistake I made further solidified my negative view of myself. I refer to it as my negative vortex. I have negative thoughts which lead to negative emotions. These negative emotions prompt negative actions. After the negative actions, I experience more negative thoughts because of what I have done. This leads to more negative emotions, which inevitably results in more negative actions. The spiral continues ever downward.

As I began to research this idea, I discovered I wasn't the first person to realize the connection between these three pillars of thoughts, emotions, and behavior. Cognitive Behavior Therapy (CBT) is one of the most common types of psychotherapy. In CBT, they have a parallel idea to my negative vortex called The Cognitive Triangle. As I worked toward self-improvement, I came across an image depicting the cognitive triangle. Here's a recreation of that image from my journal:

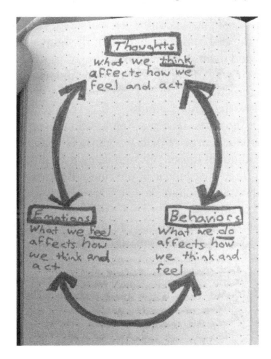

The thought that became my limiting factor was that I was not enough. This belief applied to anything that truly mattered. I knew I could perform well and put on a show. But, deep down, I was certain when someone really needed me I would let them down. In an attempt to become stronger and more resilient, I calloused my emotions to resist weakness. I would bury sadness, anger, and any negative sentiment. My lack of emotions resulted in me losing empathy. While this prevented me from feeling deep sadness, I never felt real happiness either. I never felt real peace or joy. That emptiness caused a blur of buried irritation and bitterness. These feelings weren't acute, but they were always lurking. I would contain these negative impulses when I was sober, but when I was drunk all of my inner confusion would spew out as venom toward others. The next day I would hate myself and think of nothing but all the ways I was awful. This in turn made me feel worse about myself and drove me to drink even more. The longer I ruminated, the faster I spun through this cycle until I was caught in a self-perpetuating whirlwind of negativity where there seemed to be no way out.

The scary thing about the negative vortex brought on by rumination is most people don't even realize they're in it. Either they are like me and refuse to share their thoughts with anyone, or they surround themselves with other negative people who perpetuate their way of thinking. I swirled around and around this tornado for a decade before I came to find a strategy that helped me slow the driving winds. You have to recognize and question your thoughts. It seems simple, and most people assume they're already in charge of their thoughts. We believe we analyze each thought thoroughly and categorize it neatly in the color-coded, three-ring binder of our mind. Research says we have thirty-thousand thoughts a day. That's thirty-one thoughts per minute. I assure you, you're not consciously aware of all thirty-thousand of those. More recent studies suggest we may *only* have around six-thousand thoughts a day. Still, the point remains valid. You're not catching all of those either. Becoming cognizant of the ideas swirling through your head takes concentrated practice. When you become more aware of each thought, you can stop an opinion from becoming a fact.

It's understandable to think that controlling your actions is the most reasonable method of limiting the negativity in your life. After all, you are in control of your actions. The problem with that is we stop the two or three antagonistic behaviors we wanted to commit in the day, but we allow hundreds of negative thoughts to glide on by. The fact that they are invisible to others doesn't make them any less damaging to your life. The key is to isolate our thoughts. When you can capture a negative thought, it doesn't lead to a self-deprecating emotion or an adverse behavior. When you don't have that emotion or commit that behavior, then you don't have the consequential negative thought that would have emerged from it and eventually lead to the cycle repeating itself again. Grabbing that initial thought ceases the negative vortex all together.

For the majority of us, the gun is fired to start the race of the day the moment we wake up. We rush to get ready for work or school. We busily dedicate ourselves to the day's task while also planning for what needs to be done in the future. We then return home exhausted, and the thought of reflecting on the day is the last thing on our minds. If we are to become the masters of our thoughts instead of letting our thoughts lord over us, we have to be able to accomplish this in the moment. This is achieved through mindfulness. While practicing mindfulness, we attempt to achieve a mental state where we are focused on the present moment while calmly acknowledging and accepting feelings, thoughts, and sensations. When you are mindful, you intentionally slow down your body, mind, and the world around you.

Dr. Stephen Ilardi, author of *The Depression Cure*, lays out a three-step process to end rumination and eliminate the false limiting beliefs associated with it. Step one is mindfulness. A common myth is that the goal of mindfulness is to completely clear your mind. In actuality, that is the exact opposite of the truth. Through mindfulness, you become capable of recognizing each individual thought. Then, you get to consciously decide whether to dwell on that idea or let it peacefully drift away without any emotional attachment. Like all skills, it is improved by repetition. You must become aware of when you begin to ruminate and take action against it early. This is why meditation has become such an integral part of my mental health as it is my time to practice mindfulness. I can attempt to be completely present in the moment by becoming aware of myself and my surroundings on a second-by-second basis. From this mindful state, I can head out into the world more prepared to be aware of myself and others. Meditation is my way of intentionally forcing myself to slow down and to take my attention away from productivity. It is consciously choosing my mental health over my to-do list. We often operate on autopilot, especially when performing tasks or thinking thoughts that are common to us. If it has become habitual for you to think negative thoughts, you most certainly can and will do so with little forethought or recognition.

The second step is obvious. After noticing we are beginning to ruminate, we have to choose to stop it. This part may seem like it is easy, but often it is not. When we have become accustomed to these thoughts and this process, it has most likely become ingrained. You have to rise above the weeds so you can see the entire picture. The key here is to become aware of just how much time and energy we waste through rumination. For me, it robbed me of thirteen years. When I began to accept how my thoughts were impacting my life, I was able to take back control from them.

The third and final step is to deliberately shift our attention to something else. It has to be something engaging or else our mind will wander, most likely back to whatever we were just ruminating on. The most effective way to accomplish this is through a shared activity with someone else. We can become focused on the other person and the outside world, allowing us to get out of our own head. It isn't always possible to be with someone else, so you need to find a solo activity that can fully engage your mind. It doesn't really matter what this activity is, but I strongly advise against activities that involve your phone. It is highly likely that the advertisements that are personally tailored to your tendencies and the negative influence of social media will only drive you deeper into negativity.

Now, I can accept that I am not defined by my thoughts. I can choose my thoughts in the same way I can choose my behaviors. I am not my thoughts. I am not my feelings. I am not any single action or decision. I am me. And I am exactly as God intended me to be. When I accept this to be an undeniable truth, the ideas of shame and rumination become laughable. God made me, me. And I thank Him for that.

Thoughts Action Challenge

Your thoughts aren't you any more than your arm is you. Thinking is just another physical act such as breathing or walking. It is one piece of the puzzle. Don't be taken hostage by thought. It won't be possible to notice and grab every single thought. Even so, capturing and remembering a single thought can help free you from all others: I have a choice. Whatever road I'm on, I have the choice to turn around. I choose what I live for. I choose where I focus my energy. I control my thoughts, not the other way around.

Take charge of that one thought. I have a choice. In every single thing in your life, you have a choice. Say to yourself, "I am more than my thoughts. I control my thoughts. My thoughts do not control me. I have a choice. I am not in the passenger seat of my life. I will take the wheel."

- Below, rewrite all the weaknesses that were simply opinions in the limiting beliefs action challenge. Then, I want you to write beside them what choice you will make to no longer let them negatively impact your life.

Lifestyle Change:

Another way to control your thoughts besides trying to catch and cease the negative ones is to intentionally create positive thoughts daily. I suggest doing this through a gratitude journal. Every night before bed, write out a list of things you are grateful for. I like doing mine before bed as a way to unwind from the day and to promote more restful sleep. I label it in my journal as "Blessed". On our worst days when negative thoughts consume us, we are still blessed and have so much to be thankful for. This can have an astounding impact on your health as it is a proven way to lower stress and to create a more positive outlook. A UC San Diego study showed that five minutes of gratitude journaling for eight-weeks reduced the risk of heart failure among at-risk patients.

Tonight, I want you to write down three things you are grateful for (or the way I think of it is three ways you are blessed). The more specific you are in your description, the better this process works because it forces you to truly dwell on the positive aspects of your life to find the details. For example, instead of writing "Georgia," I may write "I am thankful for Georgia's snuggles before bed because it gives us a chance to talk with no distractions."

For the next week, continue this habit by writing in a journal three things you are grateful for every night. We have so much to be thankful for if we slow down and examine all of the gifts in our lives. As you shift your mindset to one of continual gratitude, this positivity will rub off on the people closest to you as their eyes are opened to the blessings in their life as well.

<u>Lesson 18: habits are real (and you are what you repeatedly do).</u>
[23] Then he said to them all: "Whoever wants to be my disciple must deny themselves and take up their cross daily and follow me."

- Luke 9:23

[7] Do not be deceived: God is not mocked, for whatever one sows, that will he also reap.

- Galatians 6:7

Learning is more important than the test. Practice well, and the games will take care of themselves.

- Quiet Strength by Tony Dungy

Ultimately, character and its growth don't come from rules but from the small actions of responsibility that occur day after day.

- Uncommon by Tony Dungy

I started working toward self-improvement the instant I knew Hope was pregnant with Georgia because I knew there wasn't a magic wand to make me better. If I wanted to make a real change, it had to start with small, repetitive actions that I would take daily. I struggled to control my inner world, and I knew I couldn't undo a decade of pain overnight. If I wanted my anxiety to go away, I had to live my life in a way that would reduce stress. In other words, if I wanted the results, I had to put in the daily work. A goal without a plan is just a wish. For Georgia, I wasn't going to wish myself better. I was going to do something about it. Below I've listed some of the habits I've formed merely as ideas that you can consider trying. Do whatever works best for you. You are just looking for nuances you can add to your daily life to reduce stress and improve your mental health.

The first habit I highly recommend is journaling. I explained some of the benefits of writing while introducing action challenges. I believe this is the first and most crucial step in eliminating rumination. I wasn't capable of sharing my struggles with the world, but I could share them with myself.

Writing everything down became therapeutic as I finally had some sort of release for everything that had been smothering me for years. When re-reading my journal, I was able to notice patterns and trends in my thoughts that I was unaware of. It allowed me to begin to single out the thoughts I ruminated on most often and address them. I keep a pocket-sized bullet journal so I can carry it with me at all times. My entries into these journals are seen in pictures throughout this book. I include basically everything I do in these:

1. Notes as I read books, devotionals, or my Bible.
2. Daily to-do list organized by the deadline for completing each item.
   a. This helps ensure I spend my time on the most pertinent task. I have a tendency to do what I call "productive procrastination". I'm too obsessed with productivity to sit back and do nothing so I will put off tasks I dread doing by working on things that are easier to accomplish. It still has the same impact as procrastination because I have to ultimately rush to finish the task I have put off.
   b. It also allows me to be more mindful throughout the day because I can keep my mind from wandering off to analyze all the stuff I need to be getting done. I can be present in the moment. I know I will achieve the necessary objectives if I just refer back to this list I made in the morning.
   c. It gives me a stopping point for the day. When I mark the last item off the list for the day, I do not allow myself to add something else. Otherwise, I will work every single available moment of the day.
3. Prayer requests.
4. General thoughts and reflections.

A second habit that is integral for me to lessen my anxiety symptoms is having a daily session of silence with deep breathing. I often do this during guided meditation from the

Calm app, but I also implement it any time I feel myself starting to struggle with anxiety. Dr. Rangan Chatterjee suggests 3-4-5 breathing which means to take a three second inhale, hold for four seconds, and release a five second exhale. If you are exercising or in stress, the natural response is to take short, rapid breaths to supply your muscles and brain with immediate oxygen. This results in your exhales coming in quick, short bursts because your body's demand for oxygen requires you to revert back to inhaling as fast as possible. Your body interprets this as a stress signal and responds accordingly. 3-4-5 breathing has you intentionally breathe in the opposite fashion. By taking long, slow exhales you are signaling to the body that you are in a moment of peace with a lessened need for oxygen. It's medically proven that a longer exhale than inhale activates the parasympathetic nervous system to trigger your "relaxed mode". When I feel my chest getting heavy or one of my other anxiety triggers, I excuse myself from company and do this meditative breathing. It is the most actionable, effective method of immediately counteracting anxiety that I have found.

A third and final suggestion is to search for a new skill. Try out lots of things from crocheting, writing, painting, skiing, playing the guitar, or anything that interests you. The activity really doesn't matter, only that you find a hobby you can dive into. This helps on multiple levels. First, this immediately becomes your step three for stopping rumination. When you recognize a negative thought, you can divert your focus toward this activity. It is likely to maintain your attention as you are concentrating on developing your new skill. Second, it helps you to create a positive self-image. You're adding another item onto the list of things you are good at and can be proud of. Lastly, it is the external signal to yourself that you are changing and improving. It solidifies the reality that you are working toward a new life with new interests and opportunities. Seeing your mental effort take on a physical form offers reassurance that your recovery is real.

For me, the hobby I started was sketching. I was always a terrible artist. Still, I started sketching anyway because this habit isn't meant to be about achievement or perfection. It is merely something that you enjoy. I am still awful if I try to draw anything simply from my mind, but I've developed to where I'm not too bad if I have an image to replicate. When I catch negative thoughts, I sketch in my journal. The amount of attention required for sketching allows me to get lost in drawing and remove myself from the negative vortex that can swirl inside me. Psychologists refer to the immersion as flow. We see it in children all the time as they become lost in whatever activity they're doing, and it is hopeless to expect them to recognize and respond to you. This became my way to feel close with George as well. George was an amazing artist. Due to his physical limitations, he spent a lot of time in his room drawing. He was truly skilled. I have several of his pieces hanging in my room. When I sketch, I feel connected to him as I can imagine him straining over small details in his work just as I am doing.

Georgia loves drawing as well. One night when she was five, Georgia was opening up to me about her very first crush. Jokingly, I asked, "Do you love him?" She replied, "I love him, but not as much as Art." I thought she was talking about a boy named Art so I said, "Woah now. I can handle you being in love, but you are going to be limited to loving one person at a time." She looked at me confused and said, "No, art. Like coloring." Surprisingly, her first love didn't last. If only she had loved him as much as art. I hope drawing can become an activity for her where she'll think about her Bubby George as well.

This lesson contains some of his illustrations (framed) and my sketches. He loved comics and utilized color in all of his work. I'm colorblind so pencils suffice for me. I've also included a couple of my sketches after my inker, Georgia, has really brought them to life. When I originally drew the swan, I didn't realize she should have a hairbow, belt, and curly hair. Still, when you think about it, that long swan neck is just begging to be complemented by a necktie. She's a true visionary.

I am the least naturally artistic person in my immediate family besides my dad (in your face, Dad). Since I have no natural inclination toward art, I would have never attempted to sketch without my desire to connect with George. Unlike me, Georgia takes after her Bubby George and was born an artist. Today, Georgia and I will draw together while she asks questions about him. I reminisce about the man who changed my life and consequently hers. Her love of art gives us the opportunity to spend this quality time together undistracted by the outside world. Without George, we never would have had these moments I treasure so dearly. He is still guiding me and making my life better after he's been gone all these years.

George's Artwork

My sketches

These are the only two original sketches I have ever done. The hands bound by anxiety, shame, and so much more became the inspiration for the cover of this book. Jesus' hand reaching down to take the world off of the woman's shoulders was drawn for a friend who asked for a sketch personally for her.

My sketches after my inker works her magic

Habits Action Challenge

- What is something in your life you wish you were doing but are not? Or, just as importantly, what is something you are doing but know it is time for you to quit? Below, write down a habit you will start (or break) that will move you toward your desires.

Charles Duhigg in the *Power of Habit* claims creating habits is a three-step process. We'll step through them here.

1) Create a trigger - If you want to start or stop a habit, it is going to take daily repetitions. Most attempts at change end in failure because we start out so passionate, but as we become accustomed to the idea, our enthusiasm and dedication fade. It is rarely a choice to give up on the change. You miss a day here or there. Then, that single day without the action turns into a week. Eventually, it just kind of slips away. A trigger is a reminder that tells you to start the process. It is something you already have present in your life and will be the reminder to continue your habit each day. Examples would be "Before I brush my teeth I will ___." or "Everyday while I eat lunch I will ___." It works best if you pick a regular part of your schedule and add to it. The book *Life Is a Joke: 100 Life Lessons* describes the importance of a trigger perfectly. "The beauty of this is that it switches the burden from willpower to a reminder system."

   a) What will your trigger be?

2) Pick a routine - This is the action you will take (or not take) after your trigger. One example would be if you are wanting to stop smoking, your trigger may be your break at work. Normally, this would be the time you step outside to smoke and unwind. Your routine would be the

new action that you take in place of this old one. Maybe you will listen to music on your break or whatever you feel is an adequate replacement. Another example may be that you want to start taking vitamins and your trigger is to take them before you brush your teeth. In this example, the routine is simply to take the vitamin. The key here is to be specific. Something like "I will make the world a better place" is too vague and has no specific action connected. Also, it's much too large. Start small with the exact action you will take. If there are lots of things in your life you want to change, don't tackle them all at once. Too much change at one time becomes hard to maintain and results in failure for all the efforts. Start with one habit. Stick with it until it is something you naturally do in your life. Then, move on to the next.

    a)   What will your routine be?

3)   Enjoy the reward - This is simply the benefit you get from the new habit. Acknowledge each action as an important step toward making the change you want to see. You may want to work up to walking five miles, but you can only do half a mile that first day. That's still half a mile that you intentionally walked to improve your life. Make your new habit a priority, but not a job. Do it because you get to, not because you have to. At first, your reward may be simply that you are making the choice to better yourself. Relish that. Take pride in the fact that you are one of the few willing to take responsibility for your own life. To run a marathon, the first thing you have to do is take a step, and that first step is just as important, if not more so, than all of the rest.

    a)   What will be your ultimate reward when (not if) you are successful in implementing this habit into your daily life?

Lifestyle change:

Creating meaningful, lasting change in your life isn't

magic. It takes intentional care and continued application. My life is different now. I have peace, joy, and love—things I've longed for my whole life and had almost given up on ever obtaining. It did not happen overnight. Heck, you're reading a book about all the time and effort it took to get here. Each small change I made has been important to obtaining holistic wellness. If you want the changes you are working toward to last, you need a plan. Today, I want you to implement the plan you designed above and follow through with it every day for the next week. Start on the road to measurable positive change not only for yourself but for all of the people in your life.

  To make each daily attempt feel more rewarding, keep a "habit jar." Every time you follow through with your habit, put a small item into the jar (decorative rock, coin, bead, etc.). Even though you may not feel like you are making any positive change in the moment, this jar will allow you to see all of the times you took control of your life. I personally ordered 10,000 tiny pearls off of Amazon for $7. When I feel rumination starting to settle in or shame beginning to take hold, I can look at these jars and accept that the good I have done in my life far outweighs the bad. Eventually, I hope to have my home decorated with multiple mason jars filled with proof of 10,000 good decisions I made. I suggest you do the same. If you have children, have them start their own little jars. What more beautiful decoration could a home have than proof of the good you are intentionally incorporating into your lives and the world?

<u>Lesson 19: self-love is real (and she deserves what I will never have).</u>

[14] For sin shall not be master over you, for you are not under law but under grace.

- Romans 6:14

[14] I praise you, for I am fearfully and wonderfully made. Wonderful are your works; that I know very well. - Psalm 139:14

Know God. Love All. Serve Others.
- Midway Baptist Church Motto

[24] Father, you loved me before the creation of the world.
- John 17:24

I had made some incremental progress toward wellness as I poured through every resource I could find to build something resembling a holistically healthy life. Even so, I still fought the belief that no matter my efforts, I would never be enough. Accepting that I was weak and unworthy made all my striving and toil to become a better man superficial. I was working to overcome my weakness and to become enough while deep down knowing I had already lost the battle. I worked to love others. I tried showing them their beauty, worth, and importance. Even so, I never even bothered to turn those efforts inward. I believed that was futile because I was not beautiful. I was not worthy. I was not important. I never took the time to just be with myself because I didn't view myself as someone I wanted to be with. I worked without pause to become better than I was. It literally never occurred to me that maybe I was worthy of love just as I was.

I couldn't bear thinking of Georgia viewing herself this way. I can't have her growing up believing she has to be anything more than she is. I have to help her love herself for who she is rather than measure herself by her accomplishments. I ask her often, "When does Daddy love you more, when you are a good girl or a bad girl?" She replies, "Both." To which I say, "The same. All the time." I love her the same with everything in me all the time, no matter what. My hope is that if she accepts that my love for her is unconditional, then maybe her love for herself can be the same.

While reading *The Daily Office*, the book that also contained the "starting with me" passage detailed in Lesson 1, I stumbled across a viewpoint of love that was confusing to me. Bernard of Clairvus was the abbot of a Cistercian monastery in France in the 12th century. He was perhaps the greatest Christian leader and writer of his day. In his work, *Loving God*, he described the four degrees of love as:

1. Loving ourselves for our own sake
2. Loving God for His gifts and blessings
3. Loving God for Himself alone
4. Loving ourselves for the sake of God

The first three levels made sense to me. Loving ourselves for our own sake is the most shallow form of affection. It is selfish. I would argue that if your care ends there, then it isn't really love at all. The next level—loving God for His gifts—is also superficial. It is still a self-serving, egocentric form of worship. Loving God for himself alone felt like the highest possible glorification. It's why we're here in the first place. Mark 12:30 says that the greatest commandment is to love God. Seemed pretty straightforward to me.

I reflected on this passage a lot over the next couple of weeks. A lot of my trouble was probably rooted in the fact that I did not love myself so I couldn't accept that to be the greatest form of love. The longer I dwelled on this concept, the clearer it started to become. If we don't love ourselves, then we don't love the gift of life He has given us. Love what God has created. God's love for us is the most fierce, passionate emotion in existence, and we are called to love ourselves in that fashion. This is much harder than loving God for Himself alone. God is perfect. He has given us grace and redemption. We owe everything to Him. Loving Him should come quite easily. Loving ourselves on the other hand, that can be quite different. We are imperfect. We make mistakes. There are plenty of reasons not to love ourselves. The greatest form of love is to put aside all of that rationalization and love ourselves anyway. You don't love yourself because you deserve it. You do it because God deserves it.

To truly love others, you have to first love yourself. How can you give love to others if you don't have any to give? You can dedicate yourself to them in every way imaginable, but if you don't hold yourself in high esteem, you're only giving them empty deeds. It doesn't take love to offer something that is worthless. If you don't feel you have worth, whatever piece of yourself you give to others has no value either. It didn't take any real sacrifice to give it up. Mark 12:31 says the second greatest commandment is to love your neighbor as yourself. If you don't love yourself, then that is a pretty low bar to reach. If you love yourself and you are still willing to give of yourselves to others, then what you offer has importance and worth. In turn, that shows them that they too have value, or else you wouldn't be willing to give up something as special as yourself.

I came to realize that to love all, I had to also love myself. If every single person in the world deserves love, then I deserve love too because I am somebody. Loving others has to start with loving me. In that place of stillness, I can accept that I am okay and worthy of love. Only then can I return to that place to give that worth back to someone else. They are worth it because I am worth it. I am worth it because they are worth it. We are all worth it because Christ died to make us so. We are not the labels we put on ourselves. We are not a priest, a sinner, a good person, a bad person, a teacher, a student, an athlete. None of these labels have significance. We are all only children of Christ. No more and no less. Denying myself love is denying what Christ sacrificed for me. I decided to begin to try to love myself. I didn't know how I could ever accomplish that, but for God and for Georgia I could at least try.

Self-love Action Challenge

● For the next five minutes, write down all the reasons you're glad to be you, and why you wouldn't choose to be anyone else in the world.

Lifestyle change:

I gave you more writing space than normal for this action challenge. It shouldn't have taken you a long time to sit and think of positive things about yourself to write down. You should have run out of time with lots of characteristics left to write and in need several more pages to finish. If this wasn't the case, you need to think differently about yourself. Love yourself. Christ died for you, and only you can be you.

From the ages of three to five, Georgia said the same prayer every night.

"Thank you God for me. Amen."

I used to always laugh to myself about that prayer. That is, until she stopped it this year. She's six years old, and she has already stopped "thanking God for me." When was the last time you thanked God for making you who you are and not anyone else in the world? He made you to be just as you are, both the things you love about yourself and the things you hate. Everything about you was chosen with love and care to make you be the perfect realization of God's plan.

We all spend so much time trying to be something different because we are convinced we are the only people with problems. Everyone has their own issues. No life is perfect. Every day for the next week, when you wake up, I want you to say out loud (or at least think it to yourself if you think it's weird to say out loud) something about yourself that you are proud of. Start your day out with a positive self-image. From that place of self-confidence, look for the opportunity to compliment others. You never know how someone is feeling about themselves that day. Something as simple as "I like your new haircut" or "I really thought you did a good job on that presentation yesterday" may give someone the confidence boost they needed to see their own beauty, worth, and importance.

Lesson 20: peer-pressure is real (and the danger of what ifs).
[10] The thief comes only to steal and kill and destroy; I have come that they may have life, and have it to the fullest.
- John 10:10

[2] Do not conform to the pattern of this world, but be transformed by the renewing of your mind. Then you will be able to test and approve what God's will is—his good, pleasing and perfect will.
- Romans 12:2

We might be functioning out of an inordinate sense of "ought and should", burdened by unrealistic expectations about what it means to be a good Christian.
- Sacred Rhythms by Ruth Haley Barton

Comparison is the thief of all joy.
- Theodore Roosevelt

My daughter is the nerd of all nerds. She gets it honest as I am a proud nerd myself. She loves reading. Her mom has read her most of the Harry Potter series, and we're almost done with the second Artemis Fowl book here. Recently, she's started taking her school iPad with her to bed and using her class's app to read to her in addition to our nighttime reading together. She has to get several books in a night because the app keeps track of each student's progress and ranks them. One boy is ahead of her (gasp!). Obviously, she cannot stand for this and is determined to catch him. Like I said, she's a nerd.

Anyway, back before she was a six-year-old grown-up, one of our bedtime books was called *Jonathan James and the Whatif Monster* by Michelle Nelson-Schmidt. It begins by explaining that we all have a Whatif Monsters that follows us around. Whatif Monsters like to fill our heads with worry. Their whispers of doubt can change how we think. Jonathan James, the book's main character, goes on throughout the book to avoid a lot of the activities he wants to do because the Whatif Monster keeps warning him of the things that could go wrong. He wants to run a race, but the Whatif Monster worries that he may not be fast and could come in last. Jonathan James is about to jump off the diving board in front of his friends at the pool, but the Whatif Monster warns that the water may be chilly and everyone will think he looks silly. Being the sap that I am for all things Georgia, I started tearing up the first time we read this (and many times after).

Georgia asked what was wrong. I tried to explain to her what I was feeling. I told her that she was my beautiful, smart, perfect angel. Still, I knew that someday she would grow up, and she would not feel beautiful or smart. I knew someday she'd feel anything but perfect. The terrible part was that it would have nothing to do with her actual intelligence or her real beauty. I told her I was afraid she would grow up and feel ugly just because she thought someone else was prettier. I cried as I pleaded with her not to grow up and feel dumb just because she thought someone else was smarter. She was only four years old, so she just stared at me blankly. Then, her only reply was, "Can you start back reading?" The concepts of comparison, jealousy, and self-doubt were foreign and meaningless to her.

I knew one day those feelings would become all too real to her. I just didn't expect that day to come so soon. Recently, Georgia told me that she was fat and ugly. She's six. She shouldn't be worrying about her weight or her appearance. I was ready to fist fight whoever had put these thoughts into her head. Then, I realized I would have to challenge the whole world. The whole world put those thoughts into her head. So, I guess that's what I'm doing with this book. Challenging the world to be different. You better do it because if you make my daughter cry again, I'm going to hunt you down and fight you. Unless you are a lot bigger, stronger, and tougher than me. In that case, we can just talk it out. If you're feeble though, watch your back.

Honestly, society feeds these thoughts to her everywhere she looks. Everything screams to her that you have to be skinnier. You must be smarter. You have to be better. That is a crushing realization to me as her father. It is my duty to protect her from harm. It is a job I fulfill gladly. Even so, comparison and peer-pressure aren't things I can protect her from. One day, I will have to let her go out into the world on her own. All I can do is try to show her every day with everything I do that she is enough. Just as she is, she is enough. I have to let her know that it doesn't matter what the world is. The only thing that matters is who she is. She's six years old, and I'm already losing this battle.

Peer-pressure Action Challenge

- Recount a few occasions where you have let "what if" impact your decisions. In other words, how has your fear of what others may think affected your life?

Lifestyle change:

Comparison is the thief of all joy. It can only lead to two things: pride or envy. If you look around you and feel that you're better than everyone else, then pride sets in. This arrogance is a miserable, useless state of mind. If instead you believe that you're worse than others, then discontentment and envy take over. When your life is dictated by either of these two attributes, you can never be authentic because every decision you make is based on how that action will be interpreted by others.

Eventually, Jonathan James gets fed up with the Whatif Monster and all of his worries. He decides he's going to run the race and have a great time, no matter his place. He counters that what if he jumps into that pool and everyone thinks he looks really cool. In other words, the character decides to live life on his own terms instead of evaluating his actions based on what others may think. We miss out on so much in life because we are afraid of "what if". This fear has nothing to do with our own ability and everything to do with what others will think.

For this lifestyle change, I want you to pick something small. Find something you have been hesitant to do because you were afraid of failing or what others may think. Maybe you wanted to dye your hair, but you wanted an unusual color others may disapprove of. Perhaps you wanted to join a sports team, but you're afraid others may laugh at you because you are a beginner. Enough. Don't allow yourself to choose to be less than you are simply because of the opinion of others. Get rid of your Whatif Monster. Go do something today that you know you want in your life but the fear of the perception of others has held you back from.

Share this action with someone else. Even better, invite someone else along and encourage them to get rid of their own Whatif Monster. Be the stimulus to creating a world where everyone could just be who they are. What a beautiful place that would be.

Lesson 21: addiction is real (and it hurts the ones we love the most).

And Lord knows "I can't change"
Sounds better in a song
Than it does with hell to pay.
- "Sounds Better in a Song" by Drive-by Truckers

[16] For everything in the world—the lust of the flesh, the lust of the eyes, and the pride of life—comes not from the Father but from the world. [17] The world and its desires pass away, but whoever does the will of God lives forever.
- 1 John 2:16-17

[3] He heals the brokenhearted and binds up their wounds.
- Psalms 147:3

[7] All streams flow into the sea, yet the sea is never full. To the place the streams come from, there they return again. [8] All things are wearisome, more than one can say. The eye never has enough of seeing, nor the ear its fill of hearing.
- Ecclesiastes 1:7-8

When Georgia had just turned three years old, I hadn't had a drink for fourteen months in an attempt to save my marriage. Without alcohol, I avoided repeating all of the shameful, disgraceful acts I had done over the last decade. Nonetheless, Hope and I realized that even without the fighting or problems, there was an absence of love. We had both known our relationship had problems before we were ever married. We were both just vain enough to believe we would find a way to make it work anyway.

She was nice. I was nice. She was smart. I was smart. She was hard-working. I was hard-working. I knew she'd be a good mom. She knew I'd be a good dad. All of that would be enough to make things come together once we were married. Except the distance between us never narrowed. Nothing either of us ever tried helped. We were calloused toward one another. Once while we were at a show when Georgia was two, she took both of our hands in her lap and made us hold hands. Even then, she could see the lack of love. Hope and I both understood that our marriage couldn't be saved. No matter how much either of us tried to force it, we simply didn't love each other and probably never had. We mutually decided that even though we both hated to lose time with Georgia, we had to be the role-models she deserved. That meant we had to put her best interests ahead of our desires to be with her always. Most importantly, we had to be a living example of real love. If we stayed together, we couldn't do that. We accepted that a divorce was the best option and that we would split joint custody of Georgia.

During those fourteen months of sobriety, I still had the urge to drink when we were at social gatherings. I just abstained through willpower alone. Still, I didn't believe I had a problem anymore. My ability to withstand the temptation was evidence to me that I had recovered. I was not an alcoholic. Alcoholics can't keep themselves from drinking for so long, can they? I had worked for four years now toward self-improvement which rationally meant I had to be better. If you work toward something for so long, you have to eventually get there, don't you? Still, something just didn't feel right. I still never had a single moment of real peace. I had given up on joy. I don't believe I truly loved anyone in the world besides Georgia, including myself. I had put so much effort into being the man Georgia deserved, I couldn't accept that all that time had been in vain. I concluded that whatever issues I had couldn't still be my fault. Consequently, the reason for my despair had to be something external. I wasn't willing to admit I was suffering from depression. No way. Not me. I told myself I was "too normal" and "too strong" for that, but I had forgotten that conformity is cowardice. If I was depressed, it wasn't because of me. It had to be because of my marriage. Living in a hopeless, empty marriage would make anyone depressed. Right?

I had convinced myself my marriage was the problem, not my drinking. My drinking had gotten much worse during my relationship with Hope. That was true, but I conveniently ignored that it was a severe problem well before I ever met her. My anger issues did escalate dramatically during our relationship, but I disregarded the fact that I had buried my rage for years upon years. As Carlos Whittaker explains in his book

Kill the Spider, when I resisted drinking I had cleaned out the cobwebs, but I left the spider. I had only dealt with the symptoms, not the cause. I had quit drinking, but I had never rid myself of my limiting belief that I was not enough. I had never dealt with the shame I felt not only from my failure to support George but also about who I had become. I had to force a smile and fake happiness. To me, that made me a liar. No matter what I was doing, good or bad, I was always hiding a part of me, so I was a fraud.

Every year since George's death, I had developed more and more disdain for myself. I could quit drinking, but I couldn't love myself. I genuinely thought I was better though. I thought I had come into the light, but it was merely that I had been in the dark so long my eyes had acclimated to it. I had carried my burdens so long I didn't feel the weight anymore. I didn't know what I was missing because I had forgotten what loving myself felt like. It had been so long since I had felt good about myself that I didn't even realize how deeply I hated who I had become at this point.

I was certain I could drink responsibly now. After all, I had gone fourteen months without drinking so I wasn't an alcoholic or anything. Confidently, I began drinking again. Nine months later I was arrested for a DUI.

Madison Central, where I had taught for the previous nine years, was forty-five minutes from my house. After the divorce, I was solely responsible for Georgia half of the time. Even though I loved Madison Central, I had to move to a school closer to home so I could drop her off at daycare and be there in time to pick her back up. The details I shared with people about my DUI were that I met up with co-workers who had thrown me a going away party in Richmond, KY. That night after we left the bar, I tried to drive to a co-worker's house to stay the night since I lived so far away. That's all true. No lies there. It's still despicable to drive drunk, but I tried to make it seem at least somewhat understandable. I went out for drinks to celebrate our time together and got arrested trying to get to a nearby house. What I failed to mention is that I was so drunk I slipped and almost fell down the steps leaving. I also left out that slipping was my last memory before coming to almost two hours later driving. I had been driving all of that time with no recollection. I didn't share that if a little kid had wandered out into the street, there is no way I would've been able to swerve. I conveniently left out that I had to try to use Google Maps on my phone to get home even though I was in an area I had been hundreds of times. I didn't say anything about the fact that I ran a red light because I was looking at the map and almost hit a police car. I definitely didn't divulge that I blew a 0.197—more than triple the legal limit—even though I hadn't had a drink in over two hours.

The fact that I could do this to Georgia is what made me finally accept what I was. I am an addict. I am an alcoholic. I am the problem. Not my environment or my circumstances. Not anyone else. Just me.

Addiction Action Challenge

For some of us like me, our addictions are extremely visible. Everyone in my world knew of my addiction in this instant. For others, their addictions can be sneakier and easier to hide. To be able to move away from that jail cell to the place I am now, the first thing I had to do was finally accept I am an addict. From there, I had to evaluate the source of my addiction. I had to look at what drove me to want to drink to such lengths.

We have looked at my alcoholism. Still, there are countless other addictions. Food. Pornography. Nicotine. Drugs. The need for praise. Work. We can become so reliant on these addictions that we don't really see the negative impact they are having on our lives until it's too late. I had found a way to ignore all the signs screaming I was an alcoholic until the reality was forced down my throat.

- This will take some honest, deep self-reflection. It will take much more than this single action challenge to remove this addiction from your life, but step one is acknowledging the problem. If your addiction is more subtle, you could be in denial that you have an addiction at all. Look back at the "Great Exchange" from the Lesson 15 (purpose) Action Challenge. You should have tried to prevent yourself from doing something in order to honor what you care about the most. If you are still committing that act, no matter what it is, even though you have consciously tried to stop it for the thing you love the most in the world, then you are addicted to it. I assure you the idea that you can isolate this addiction from the rest of your life is a lie. Our addictions impact every part of us in some way. Is there something in your life you have an addiction to? If you feel the word addiction is too strong, then is there something in your life that you have an unhealthy reliance on? Explain.

Lifestyle change:

For the majority of you, your hang-up is not as visibly damaging to your life as mine was. Even so, that doesn't mean it can't be just as devastating. I believe our addictions to our phones is the most common and silently detrimental addiction in society today. There are more mobile devices on planet Earth than people (Dr. Rangan Chaterjee - *How to Make Disease Disappear*). One study in 2014 of 2,000 people in the UK found we check our phones 221 times a day and spend on average three hours and sixteen minutes on them. A statistic from the US estimates that the average user touches their phone 2,617 times per day. Our brains release small amounts of dopamine in response to text messages, likes on our social media posts, and so forth. Dopamine is essentially your "happy" neurotransmitter. We become physically addicted to this need for comfort and reassurance.

Today, I want you to put your phone away in another room or somewhere physically away from you for just an hour or two. Encourage the others you are with to do the same. Then, just live life. Do whatever you want. Just be present in the moment with the people around you. I have to do the same thing when I play with Georgia. If my phone is around me, I am checking on Philadelphia Eagles information or scouring the fantasy football waiver wire for the third time that day. Quite simply, the vast majority of us are severely addicted to our phones. Remove the temptation for this brief period of time. I've found that I crave these times where I can get away from emails, social media, and all the other distractions I find for myself through my phone.

Lesson 22: shame is real (and it is the enemy of joy).
[12] For I will forgive their wickedness and will remember their sins no more.

- Hebrews 8:12

Persecution forced the believers out of their homes in Jerusalem, and along with them went the gospel. Sometimes we have to become uncomfortable before we'll move. We may not want to experience it, but discomfort may be best for us because God may be working through our hurts. When you are tempted to complain about uncomfortable or painful circumstances, stop and ask if God might be preparing you for a special task.

- Life Application Study Bible

Last night I did myself a favor
I called in sick and went downtown
Drove past a local bar
A cop got behind my car
I wish he would pull me over now
Last night I let myself remember
Times I forgot a woman's name
I blacked out behind the wheel
How tight the handcuffs feel
My daughter's eyes when she's ashamed

- "It Gets Easier" by Jason Isbell

I am an alcoholic, but that was only the mechanism for my true vices of avoidance and denial. I could not accept the things that had happened in my life. Alcohol was simply the most effective tool I used to run from these thoughts. In combination, my avoidance and alcohol had led me to the concrete floor of a jail cell in Richmond, KY. Everyone in the town knew about my arrest before I was ever released. Everyone knew how pathetic I was. The mask I wore to cover my weakness for so long had been forcibly ripped away.

I woke up in jail at 7:00 a.m. Typically, after a DUI, you are released relatively early the next day after you are sober. There were problems reaching a judge to approve my release, so I stayed in jail until 1:00 a.m. the following morning. For twenty-two hours, I lay on the floor surrounded by criminals. A homeless man lay beside me who was in jail for beating his girlfriend in public. He called me "Teach" the whole day because I was a teacher. One man was in holding after his fourth DUI. He was to be put in jail for four years the next day. There was a father and son duo who had been arrested for selling heroin. The son claimed he was going to murder his ex-wife when he got out for turning them in. And I was one of them. I was right where I deserved to be. I had risked the lives of innocent people by driving drunk. I was a criminal too. My life had fallen apart in an instant.

I tried to call my brother to come pick me up, but he was asleep. I didn't have my phone, and the only other number I had memorized was my parents' home. Using the jail's phone, I had to call my dad at midnight to wake him up and tell him that I had been arrested. Again. I had to tell the man I admire more than anyone else in the world that my life was in shambles and that I had let him down. Again. I had to tell him I was a disappointment. Again.

My dad was able to reach my brother. Together, they drove an hour and fifteen minutes to bail me out of jail. Nobody said much on the drive back to my parents' house in my hometown of Clay County. They tried to comfort me, but there was really no solution to this situation. I had just destroyed my life so there wasn't much to say. I couldn't stop thinking about what I had done to Georgia. It was just me and her now. I had become what I always knew I was: unworthy of her. What if I had died in a crash? What if I lose my job because of the DUI? If I lose my job, then she loses her home. I had disregarded my responsibilities as a father and as a human. Even though she was too young to express it, she had a difficult enough time already processing our divorce nine months prior. She had started wetting the bed again for a couple of weeks once her mom moved out. My purpose in life was to be her Daddy and her protector, but I let her down again and again.

The next morning, it was hard for me to look Georgia in the eye. She had been staying with my parents and had no idea what had happened. The instant she woke up she ran to put her arms around my neck. She said, "You are the best daddy in the world." I know God gave me that moment of reprieve from my suffocating shame. Even so, with a tear in my eye I just had to say, "No, baby. I am not." I set her down, and she went on her way to play. I went inside to try to figure out how I was going to keep her world from falling apart.

I had struggled my entire adult life, but all of that adversity had been internal. My DUI was my first prolonged, public disgrace. I could not hide from it or rationalize it. It broke me. I hit absolute rock bottom. My anxiety and depression had been lurking in the background for a decade, but they were subdued enough that I could grit through it. With this latest disgrace adding to my other issues, my mental health problems sharply intensified. Within a week of my arrest, I began to have episodes where I struggled to breathe. Within two weeks, I started going through spells where I felt on the verge of gagging as if I were about to swallow my tongue. By the end of the first month, these symptoms were nearly constant. My chest always felt like it was caving in. I was in a perpetual state of mild suffocation. I felt a gagging sensation at all times. My symptoms were present nearly every second of every day for the next year.

My arrest came six days before the start of the school year. Like I said, the night of my DUI I was at a going away party thrown by my former co-workers. I was at a new school now where no one knew me. I didn't have nearly a decade's worth of positive reputation built up to weigh against my DUI like I would have had at my old school. I was just the new teacher who was irresponsible enough to get arrested less than a week before school began. For the first month, I lived in fear every day that I would be fired. I had to carry Georgia's car seat into school because I couldn't drive. Every day, carrying that car seat was a reminder of how much I did not deserve her. I would try to run to my class and hide it so no one would see me. It was the most humiliating thing I've ever had to do in my life. It was proof I was an unfit father. I wasn't fit to be a role model. If my daughter was ever going to have a hero like George, it wouldn't be me.

This debilitating anxiety and shame was the crescendo of a note that had started thirteen years before. I had one chance at the greatest test of my life. I failed. I left George on that beach feeling like he was not enough. The man I owe so much of my life to needed me one time. Just once. And I let him down. He died two weeks later. It was a test I could not retake.

Even during my efforts toward recovery, this had shaped everything I had done. I was convinced of my unquestionable guilt of a crime that could not be corrected or forgiven. I had lived the rest of my life knowing I would ultimately let everyone down. Finally, here was the proof. The truth I had avoided for so long and drank so much to silence was there for everyone to see. I was not enough. I was not enough to save George. I was not enough to save my marriage. I would never be enough. I would let down everyone I loved and everyone who depended on me. I was worthless.

Over the next year, I distanced myself from basically everyone. I stayed home by myself when I didn't have Georgia. It was extremely difficult to mask my symptoms when I was attempting to carry on a personal conversation, so I intentionally avoided situations where I may have to talk with anyone. Even through this, I never opened up to anyone to ask for support. I never sought professional help. I felt my struggles were my penance. I deserved all of this and more.

I couldn't just give up. I was pathetic. That much was certain, but I had been given too much to just quit. A couple months into my self-enforced exile, I saw a Ted Talk by Brené Brown entitled "The Power of Vulnerability". She was talking about her research into the impact of shame, vulnerability, courage, and empathy. Finally, after all these years, she made me realize what I was doing to myself by harboring all of my shame. Even though I instinctively knew how much damage I was causing myself, having it presented in a data driven fashion appealed to my scientific mind. Here was a doctor who had performed trials studying how the lives of those who hold to shame differed from those who do not. She explained that shame is not guilt. Shame is a focus on self while guilt is a focus on behavior. Guilt is "I did something bad." Shame is "I am bad." If you do something hurtful to someone, guilt is saying, "I am sorry. I made a mistake." Shame says, "I am sorry. I am a mistake." She said that shame is highly correlated to addiction, depression, suicide, violence, bullying, aggression, and eating disorders. Where there is shame, there can be no joy. In her words, if you put shame in a petri dish, it needs three things to grow exponentially: secrecy, silence, and judgment. I had fed my shame an unlimited supply of these ingredients for a third of my life. My shame had grown and grown until there was room for nothing else in my life.

Shame Action Challenge

- No one else ever has to read this challenge but you. It is vitally important that you begin to open up about your shame. As your first step, just be honest with yourself. What are you most ashamed of? How has this made you feel about yourself?

Lifestyle change:

Now, I want you to accept that secrecy, silence, and self-judgment can only make that thing you are so ashamed of more powerful. It only fuels the fire that smothers out your life. I know that simply asking you to throw back the curtain on the things you are ashamed of in your life isn't going to force you to do so. Instead of asking you to reveal what you are ashamed of to others, I want to ask you to be real with yourself. If you ever want a chance to be free of the grip this shameful act has on your life, then you must rid yourself of the secrecy. You must speak out against the silence. Be brave enough to face the judgment. The absolute only way you will ever completely move past this shame is to share it with someone. That isn't just my opinion. It is a scientifically supported fact. What to do with that fact is now your decision. Just know almost all of us are holding shame. The reason we cling to it so tightly is our certainty that we are alone in our shame. Somebody has to be brave enough to speak out first. And, you are somebody...

<u>Lesson 23: guilt is real (and it can be a good thing).</u>
⁹ He will not always accuse, nor will He harbor his anger
forever; ¹⁰ He does not treat us as our sins deserve or repay us
according to our iniquities. ¹¹ For as high as the heavens are
above the earth, so great is His love for those who fear him; ¹² as
far as the east is from the west, so far has He removed our
transgressions from us. As a father has compassion on his
children, so the Lord has compassion on those who fear him.
- Psalms 103:9-13

Your love never fails and never gives up.
It never runs out on me.
- "One Thing Remains" by Jesus Culture

At the end of the last lesson, I discussed Brené Brown's findings that shame is highly correlated to addiction, depression, suicide, violence, bullying, aggression, and eating disorders. Most people correlate the emotions of guilt and shame so it would seem logical that guilt would have the same impact. In actuality, guilt is negatively related to every single issue in that list. The ability to hold something up that we've done against who we want to be is actually incredibly adaptive.

My constant reflection and critique of myself wasn't the poison I felt it was. Quite the opposite. It is healthy. It is necessary. All successful people analyze where they are in life against where they want to be and make a plan to bridge that gap. Instead, the venom was merely that when I compared myself to the person I wanted to be, I was ashamed of the deep, dark cavern between those two people. Based on these results, if I had merely been able to express my presumed shortcomings with others openly, I would've actually grown rather than spiraling into the husk of a person I had become. The fear of others finding out about our faults—not the faults themselves— is the kryptonite to a holistically healthy life. In our effort to hide our guilt, we cultivate shame. We lose the ability to admit mistakes and grow from them.

Through her six years of research, Professor Brown found there was one major characteristic consistently present in people who have a sense of love and belonging that is absent in those who do not. People who had a sense of love and belonging believed they were worthy of it while those who did not lacked this assurance. That's it. The secret is just finding the belief within ourselves that we are worthy. This isn't just a colorful bumper sticker that says "Love Yourself". This is one of the predominant researchers on the impact of shame saying that my limiting belief that I was not enough was the source of my struggles. Maintaining a similar ideology to mine was the single most predictive characteristic of everyone who felt unworthy and unloved.

All my years of trying to force myself to become enough were simply compounding my problems. When you start from a place of unworthiness, no result is going to change that mindset. Failure supports your theory while any success is disregarded as an outlier or diversion from the truth. I finally had to accept that I couldn't work hard enough to become worthy. I couldn't be strong enough to become deserving. I couldn't want it enough to become valuable. If I was ever going to feel that I was worthy, I just had to accept that I am enough. I had to believe I was worthy of love regardless of my actions. It wasn't enough to clean up the outside. For the first time in my life, I vowed to truly face my darkest fears. I decided that I am enough.

After watching Brené Brown's video, I slowly began to open up the tiniest bit about my struggles. I talked to a couple family members about George's death. I didn't divulge my decade plus of mental health struggles, but I at least started sharing that I too feel pain. That seems silly to write. Of course I feel pain, but I had never told anyone about my suffering or asked for help in dealing with it. I still was not courageous enough to share my true self without inhibition. My apprehension toward vulnerability had been built over thirteen years. It wasn't a wall I could tear down all at once to expose myself completely in my raw nakedness.

Despite my efforts to reach out to others, I was still experiencing my anxiety symptoms without reprieve. Every second of every day, I struggled to breathe and fought through a gagging sensation. Even so, I was taking baby steps to accepting vulnerability as an essential component of a healthy life. I was working to rid myself of shame and share my guilt with others.

My life had faded so far from what I wanted to be that this miniscule progress might mean it would take a lifetime for me to reach where I wanted to be. Still, I was moving in the right direction for the first time since I was a nineteen-year-old kid. If it took a lifetime to get there, at least it would be an existence spent working toward something real.

I was in the middle of this transition when I went on a mission trip to La Florida, Peru in the summer of 2019. Overall, I was gone for ten days. This was the longest I had ever been away from Georgia. To compound my distress of being removed from Georgia, the Educational Professional Standards Board was reviewing my DUI. It had been a year since my arrest, but the processing of my case was still not complete. After an initial analysis of my case, it was turned over to an advisory board to determine an appropriate punishment. Typically, a first time DUI does not result in the revoking of a teacher's license, but my situation was more severe due to the additional Public Intoxication arrests in my past. The decision for my case was supposed to be posted on my second day in Peru, but there still was no news on day six. With each passing day, I was becoming more and more certain I had taught my last class. At that time, outside of becoming a cardiac surgeon in direct response to George's death, I had never considered another occupation in my entire life. I was scared of what would happen to Georgia because my degree only applied to teaching. I was unqualified for any other career. I was on the verge of being in the position I had tried to prevent for my students for over a decade: jobless without the proper training to be attractive to any prospective employer. On top of that, I would be searching for a new career with multiple alcohol-related arrests. Georgia would lose her home and would be the victim of yet another drastic change in her life. I knew how tough lack of stability can be on a child, and I was directly responsible for continually hurting my angel.

The worst part of all is that even though Georgia did not deserve this, I did. I deserved to lose my job. I had behaved in a manner unfit to serve as a role model for kids. I knew to be the person I wanted to become, I had to rid myself of shame. Even so, how can I not be ashamed when I have done so many shameful things? How do I accept guilt for my actions but avoid the shame that accompanies them?

Guilt Action Challenge

- List some mistakes you've made in the last week below. I want these to be small mistakes that do not have severe consequences.

- The only way to move toward accepting the guilt for your wrongdoings but rid yourself of the shame is to speak with someone. Anyone. Below, list the people you are willing to be open with and to show more of the real you.

Lifestyle change:

I promise you I understand how hard this is. In my opinion, it is the hardest lifestyle change in the entire *Love Is Real* Series. Nonetheless, if you truly want to move forward to a healthier, joy-filled life, then sharing your struggles is the most essential factor. You don't necessarily have to share with the people you are personally close to. It can be a therapist or literally a random person. Whoever. Just talk to someone. Open up about mistakes and regrets in your life. Start with the small ones you listed above. Eventually, I hope you build enough confidence that you can return to the Shame Action Challenge. When you build to the level where you can share those deeply shameful admissions listed there with others, then your life can truly begin.

Lesson 24: eternal peace is real (and it starts today).
[15] ...But as for me and my house, we will serve the Lord.
- Joshua 24:15

[13.] All these people were still living by faith when they died. They did not receive the things promised; they only saw them and welcomed them from a distance, admitting they were foreigners and strangers on earth... [16.] Instead, they were longing for a better country—a heavenly one. Therefore God is not ashamed to be called their God, for he has prepared a city for them.
- Hebrews 11:13 and 11:16

A child does not grow up thinking, "What's wrong with the environment where I am growing up?" They think, "What's wrong with me?"
- Emotionally Healthy Spirituality by Peter Scazzero

But a role model in the flesh provides more than inspiration; his or her very existence is confirmation of possibilities one may have every reason to doubt, saying, "Yes, someone like me can do this."
- Sonia Sotomayor

If my Daddy can do it, I can do it.
- Georgia Reid

On our seventh day in Peru, my anxiety symptoms were as severe as I have ever experienced. Generally, I could tolerate my difficulty breathing by taking deep, gasping breaths periodically. This at least allowed me to function in a manner where others didn't see me physically struggling. On this day, I was barely managing to remain upright. The heaviness of my chest made it nearly impossible to breathe. The lack of oxygen was making me feel weak and dizzy.

That day, I was responsible for shoveling sand for the concrete mixer and wheelbarrowing the concrete into a home for the floor. These were the two most physically taxing jobs on our work site. In response to my physical struggles, I fell back onto the only response I've ever really known. I decided to just fight back. I began working feverishly in intentional opposition to my anxiety. Sometimes, I'd get caught up in the line to drop off the concrete and would have to hurry back to shovel, gasping for breath. The guy I was shoveling with noticed me nervously watching to make sure I got back before anyone else could pick up the shovel, and he commented on it. It was embarrassing because I was trying to serve from my strength, not God's. I wasn't focused on loving Melissa, a single mother of two who waited for six years for this home. I wasn't working to grow as a missionary team and to serve God as a unified family. In that moment, like so many others, I had shut out the rest of the world and was in a battle with myself. I was determined to work up to and beyond my physical capacity as a personal challenge.

Like I had for much of my life, I was giving without loving. I was working for my own selfish need to show my anxiety that it couldn't stop me. I was greedy for admiration from my fellow missionaries because I could physically exert myself for so long. I was fixated on holding the most physically-demanding job the entire day simply because I could. I had flown thirty-three hundred miles away from home, but I hadn't gone far enough to get away from who I truly was. I was selfish. Despite all my outward giving, everything was still about me. The people we were building homes for had nothing. Their original homes were bamboo huts. The whole community shared a bathroom that was a bamboo-enclosed hole dug in the ground. Even though my needs were nothing compared to theirs, I was still focused on myself.

That evening, as we did every night, our team gathered for a session we eloquently called "Happies and Crappies" where we would share our personal wins and losses for the day. I had started pulling back my mask slightly to share real struggles with people. Even so, I still had not grown to the point where I could expose my deep wounds or my flawed mindset. Consequently, I had pre-determined to not share my mental struggles from the day with the team. I would do what I had done my whole life. I'd share something that sounded good to everyone else. I would share a "happy" that made me seem compassionate and loving. I would detail a "crappy" that sounded as if I was revealing a true letdown, and I would be commended for my honesty. I would appear deeply introspective and willing to be vulnerable, but everything I unveiled would simply be surface level truths that ultimately meant nothing to me. Everyone would leave feeling like they knew me, yet none of them really would.

During the meeting, my girlfriend Sarah[4] sent me a video she had taken of Georgia lifting foam weights. As she curled her toy dumbbells, Georgia said "If my daddy can do it, I can do it." That singular moment is when it all finally clicked for me. If her daddy can do it, she can do it. Here's a picture of her from the video.

I have no doubt my daughter will be a worldly success. She is smart and has positive examples in her mother and me, as well as her step-parents, that will help hone her potential. I used to worry about her work ethic (Side note: If you want to know how obsessed I am with the importance of productivity and work, I was worried about my 3-year-old daughter's work ethic). My baby is not one for physical exertion. When she had just turned two, I decided we would take a walk around a half-mile

---

[4] *She's my wife now. She's pretty awesome. Continue with us to book two of the series, Love Redeems. You'll meet her next.*

loop in our neighborhood. About fifty feet into the walk, she said she was too tired to keep going and demanded I carry her. I refused. This was her response.

She just lay face-first on the sidewalk in peaceful protest, refusing to take another step.

My worries about her growing up without dedication to working hard ended when we went on a hike with the FCA group I sponsored at Madison Central. She had walked about two-hundred feet before making me carry her. She rode on my shoulders the rest of the four-mile hike and complained about her legs being tired. Refer to Exhibit A for proof.

As you can tell from the picture, even though she was riding on my back the whole way, she was not living her best life. I was telling her that she had to learn to work hard, and it was unacceptable to be lazy. She told me, "Not everybody has to like what you like, Daddy. I work hard at my coloring." That was a wake-up call for me because I could picture my mom out there on the hike. She hates all things sweat-related. She may have followed Georgia's lead of making me carry her or lying down face-first on the trail. Yet, my mom is one of the hardest-working people I have ever met. Georgia was right. Not everybody has to like what I like. I am confident she will apply herself and work hard toward her passions. She will succeed at anything she decides to pursue. I have no doubt of it.

But in Peru, I realized how much more she would learn from me than work ethic. If her daddy can do it, she can do it. Georgia thought she was just talking about lifting weights, but she wasn't. That mindset is how she was going to live her life. Often, when I ask her what she believes about something, she'll reply, "What do you think? Because I think whatever you think." She will have grit because I have it. She will spend her life dedicated to loving others because I do. But she will also judge herself harshly and leave no room for personal mistakes because I do. She will measure herself by what she does rather than who she is because I do. She will swallow every hint of fear, doubt, and vulnerability because I do. If I want her to have the things that matter in life—love, joy, and faith—I have to show her those things are real. If I want her to have a life of peace, I have to find it for myself.

Peace and contentment had eluded me for so long. In the Lesson 17 (purpose) Action Challenge, I asked you to put Post-It Notes up for the thing that you wanted the most. Like every other action challenge, I have done that myself. You may expect that I would've had Georgia or love on my notes, but I didn't. The word peace is posted all around my house still today. It was the one thing I had never had in my whole life.

Since my earliest memories, I had to do more; I had to be more. Dad deserved it. George deserved it. Most of all, Georgia deserved it. There was always more to accomplish to earn the gift of knowing these people. I didn't have time for peace.

I actually wore my lack of peace around my neck. Shortly after my arrest, I got these dogs tags.

The one with Georgia's name says "07-27-18" because that was the day of my DUI. Mark 12:30-31 says that the greatest commandment is to love God with everything in you and the second is to love your neighbor as yourself. I never take these dog tags off. They are my constant reminder that I will never drink again. I was drunk when I made every mistake I mention in this book. I was drunk for about 95% of the mistakes I've made in my life. I haven't drank since that night. As of the time I am writing this passage, that has been 2 years, 3 months, and 20 days. The purpose of the dog tags is to remind me that if I am going to be who God and Georgia deserve, I simply cannot drink. If I ever drink again, then I love myself more than I love Georgia. If I can't love her as much as I love myself, then I cannot love anyone that much. Still, these dog tags had become more of a scarlet letter than a loving reminder. Essentially, they told me that I am a screw-up. They reminded me that I am a terrible person, and I have to fight to not be what I am. They were another reminder that there was no time for peace. I needed to work to atone for my mistakes.

While I watched that video of Georgia lifting her little weights, I accepted that I was going to have a daughter who would grow up to be successful in everyone's eyes but her own. Georgia was going to grow up to love everybody but herself. If her daddy can do it, she can do it.

It wasn't going to be my example of grit or hard-work that mattered in her life. She needed me to be her example of loving oneself and living a life of peace. I had to obtain peace for myself so Georgia could have the life I wanted for her. In that moment, my dog tags took on a new meaning. Now, they are a reminder that for me to fulfill Mark 12:30 and love God, I have to embrace the greatest form of love. I have to love myself for God. I have to love me, the good and the bad. Then, and only then, can Mark 12:31 (loving my neighbor as myself) truly make a difference in the world. I finally accepted vulnerability in its entirety. I told the group that my crappy for the day was my insistence on self-reliance and my selfish mindset. I told them I had been waiting all week to hear if I would lose my job and Georgia would lose her home. I told them about me. The real me. I told them because if her daddy can do it, she can do it.

After sharing with the team, I felt renewed the next day. Below is my unedited journal entry from the next day - June 18th, 2019:

"Today, I had a very unimportant job on the work site. I basically just reset the electricity and handed stuff to people. And, for the first time in my life, I was okay with that. The other team unexpectedly had to work concrete and shovel all day. Both are extremely physically taxing which I would normally view as my responsibility to prove myself. But, I was able to appreciate them without depreciating our group. I met a little girl named Deli who reminded me so much of Georgia (4-years old, super cute, strong-willed). For the first time the reality of Peru hit me. I've been worried about my job and Georgia losing her home. This little girl had been living in a bamboo hut with no water or electricity her whole life. And, it was still obvious the bond her and her mother have. Georgia will always love me, and I will

always love her. It doesn't matter where we are. Life is bigger than a home, work ethic, productivity, or status. Enjoy life second by second. I don't have to control it. I don't have to perfect it. I don't have to carry the weight of the world constantly. I'm wasting my life away. I'm wasting what Christ did for me. John 13:1. He loved me til the end. He died for me while I was still his enemy. I don't have to earn it. I just have to live a joyful, faithful life to honor it."

I found peace with my situation in that moment and finally understood what we were there to do. Not to fix the people of Peru's lives. They didn't need fixing. They had love and enjoyed life. I vowed to learn from them so I could do the same. I accepted my guilt for my DUI and the countless mistakes in my life, but I refused to hide them in shame anymore. From that day forward, I have been open and honest about my mental health issues. I threw off the chains of shame and accepted vulnerability. I am not perfect. Far from it. I mess up all the time, but when I mess up, I take responsibility for that mistake and work toward forgiveness. I am proud to say from that day to this one, I have lived the life that I want for Georgia. I have removed the mask that hid my shame for a third of my life. I have come to peace with who I am. I wasn't made to be George or my dad. I was made to be me.

Whoever believes in God's Son has eternal life. He is all you need. You don't need to wait for eternal life because it begins the moment you believe. You don't need to work for it because it is already yours. You don't need to worry about it because you have been given eternal life by God himself—and it is guaranteed. God doesn't do love. God is love. God's love had been with me my whole life even when I had blinded myself to it. George held to faith until his death, but his healing never came. He did not receive the things promised, but only saw them from a distance. Ultimately, he was at peace with God's plan because he was a foreigner on this Earth longing for a better country. He has now received his healing in his true home. And I have received my peace here on Earth.

I had spent my life surrounded by people but always alone. I kept the door to my life locked and bolted shut. I opened the door to allow in the love of God and the peace of surrendering to His plan. With that, I was able to restore love for myself and the world. I'm never closing that door again.

For me, an eternity of peace and a life filled with authentic love started that day.

Eternal Peace Action Challenge

If you have kids, they are watching when you do not realize it. Statistically, they are extremely likely to be what you are. That can be intimidating. No one is perfect all the time. Still, you can take intentional efforts to be a positive role-model for your kid. Georgia amazes me every day with her innate kindness and intelligence, but she needs someone to guide her and cultivate those natural gifts. Your kid does too. One activity I highly recommend is going through these three questions every night before bedtime. They were created by Charles Poliquin, a strength coach who's trained Olympic medalists in over 20 different sports.

1) What have you done on purpose today to make someone else happy?
2) What has someone else done today to make you happy?
3) What have you learned?

This ensures love will be a daily part of your lives. Georgia automatically goes into these questions every night now. I sometimes suspect it is part of her scheme to get to stay up later, but I don't mind. If intentionally reflecting on her day in a mindset of gratitude and humility means she pushes bedtime back by ten minutes, that is a trade I'll make any day. She always starts by saying, "What did I do today to make someone happy?" In a hushed voice, she'll follow that by immediately whispering, "Not on purpose." She cracks up as I feign being upset because she didn't do it on purpose. She'll say, "What?! I am always having too much fun, so I forget to do it on purpose." It's an honest reflection that if we don't make an intentional effort to help others, then we most often allow our day to just zip on by without ever trying to make someone else's world better. She'll remember our little running joke as she gets older though. My hope is that sometimes she'll think about it during the day, and it'll be her reminder to take enough time to try to help someone else (And this time, on purpose).

- If you have children, try this out with them. Even if you don't, try this out with a partner, close friend, or family member. For the three questions above:

Your Answers:
1)

2)

3)

Their Answers:
1)

2)

3)

- I realize some of you do not have kids so you may feel like a lot of this role-model stuff doesn't apply to you. You don't have kids watching your every move, so you're off the hook. Hopefully you've stuck it out and are still reading at this point anyway. That's a good thing because the truth is everyone is a role model. Our children are not the only people looking to us to see how they should live their lives. Below, I want you to write out a list of all the people who could possibly look up to you. Some suggestions would be little brothers/sisters, nieces/nephews, friends, cousins, work peers, etc.

Read through the list you just made. Now, I want you to accept that there are other people in the world looking to you who you do not expect. There are many more people who you would've never thought to put on that list who look at the life you live. I know it for a fact. It may be your parents, your boss, or literally any person in your world.

I'll share with you how I can be so confident this is true.

My brother is twenty-six months older than me. That means our ages are just close enough that we were always competing, but just far enough apart that I was never able to win. Growing up, he was always bigger, always stronger, always faster. We would fight, and he would hold me down and perform the classic "quit hitting yourself" routine. He'd make me promise I'd quit fighting before he'd let me up, but the second he was off of me, I would start swinging wild punches again. He'd have to pin me once more because I would never quit fighting. This would repeat until eventually he'd have to run to the door and lock me out of the house to keep from having to beat me up anymore. We fought a lot when we were young, and no one would've thought I looked up to him for anything. Especially not him. Still, my brother was cool and he got girls. I wanted to be cool and get girls too. My brother always cuffed his sleeves when he wore button-up shirts. So, on my first day of high school, I cuffed my sleeves too. I would have eaten a dog turd before I would have admitted I was cuffing my sleeves because he did, but that's why I did it. To this day, every single time I wear a button-up shirt, I cuff my sleeves because my brother did it when I was fourteen. He didn't know I cared what he wore, but I did. The people you care about are looking to you for how to approach life. Are you living the kind of life you would want for them? I assure you, you are pushing them toward the same road you are on today. Your possessions, status, and power will mean nothing in God's kingdom, but you will spend eternity with other people. Invest your time and talents where they will make an eternal difference. Live a life of love. There's someone out there who needs you to.

Lifestyle change:
    The "do as I say, not as I do" line parents feed kids is absurd. If you do not live the things you preach, then they won't either.
    Not only has my eternity already begun, but so has yours and everyone else's. The life we live here determines where that eternity will be spent, and my actions have an enormous impact on the decisions my daughter will grow to make. Last week, Georgia asked me, "Besides your Bible, what's your favorite

thing?" It was comforting to me that she innately knew the importance of the Bible in my life. She knows I wake up and read while she still sleeps. She also understands that I wake up an hour early to do this because I love her, and I don't want to lose time with her by reading during the day. Without me telling her, she knows both of these things. She knows I prioritize her right along with the most important thing in the world to me. She sees her importance and the influence of Christ on my life not only because I tell her but because I show her. She is watching me even when I don't realize she is. I don't want to just bring Georgia up in church. I want to bring her up in Christ. If faith in Christ is real, it will prove itself in my home and in my relationships with those who know me best.

I had amazing parents who showed me what it means to love your child. I know many of you did not. You are trying to show your kid the right way even though you didn't have anyone to show you. You may have had parents who were abusive, emotionally distant, struggling with addiction, or any number of things that could have hurt you and your development. Be the person you always needed but maybe never had.

Almost always, those who grow up in difficult homes pledge that they will not repeat the behavior destroying their family. They will not put their kid through what they went through. Statistics show these intentions aren't enough. It takes more than willpower to overcome the negative example that has been set for you. The cycle of abuse, addiction, or whatever affliction will continue to hurt your family generation after generation unless you put a stop to it now. 51% of adults who were abused as children experience domestic abuse later in life as well (ons.gov.uk). Child abuse and neglect have a direct effect on adult intimate partner violence perpetration for men. In other words, boys who were abused or neglected are more likely to become abusive with their partners in adulthood. This is just one example. Kids whose parents abuse drugs are more likely to use than children who are not exposed to this. Children whose parents leave their life are more likely to abandon their kids as well.

You have to break the cycle. Children don't think, "What is wrong with the environment I'm growing up in?" They think, "What's wrong with me?" There are so many kids out there growing up certain that they are a mistake. They don't know enough to question the world around them. If you want a better life for your child, you must be intentional. Their eternity starts today. Your influence will greatly impact their forever.

I didn't know I was colorblind until somebody told me when I was six. I thought trees were entirely green—trunk, branches, and leaves—until I learned about photosynthesis later in grade school. I thought the green light on a stop light was white until I had my permit and was almost ready to get my driver's license. I thought the light was white but they called it the green light because green and go both start with a "g." I know that sounds foolish, but I distinctly remember being sixteen years old and asking my mom why they call the white light green. She simply said, "Because it's green." I replied, "Well, that's a pretty good reason." We all just assume what we experience is "normal" and that everybody else is experiencing the same thing. If you want your kid to have the life you didn't have, you have to show them the way. We often say we will die for our children, but we're called to do something much braver: truly live for them. Start eternity for you and your family today by devoting your life fully to Christ. Allow Christ to guide you today and every day.

Lesson 25: love is real (and no one can take it away).

[10] Each of you should use whatever gift you have received to serve others, as faithful stewards of God's grace in its various forms. [11] If anyone speaks, they should do so as one who speaks the very words of God. If anyone serves, they should do so with the strength God provides, so that in all things God may be praised through Jesus Christ. To him be the glory and the power for ever and ever. Amen.

- 1 Peter 4:10-11

[5] For this very reason, make every effort to add to your faith goodness; and to goodness, knowledge; [6] and to knowledge, self-control; and to self-control, perseverance; and to perseverance, godliness; [7] and to godliness, mutual affection; and to mutual affection, love. [8] For if you possess these qualities in increasing measure, they will keep you from being ineffective and unproductive in your knowledge of our Lord Jesus Christ. [9] But whoever does not have them is nearsighted and blind, forgetting that they have been cleansed from their past sins.

- 2 Peter 1:5-9

[7] Beloved, let us love one another, because love is from God; everyone who loves is born of God and knows God. [8] Whoever does not love does not know God, for God is love.

- 1 John 4:7-8

[12] No one has ever seen God; but if we love one another, God lives in us and his love is made complete in us.

- 1 John 4:12

[16] And so we know and rely on the love God has for us. God is love. Whoever lives in love lives in God, and God in them. [17] This is how love is made complete among us so that we will have confidence on the day of judgment: In this world we are like Jesus. [18] There is no fear in love. But perfect love drives out fear, because fear has to do with punishment. The one who fears is not made perfect in love. [19] We love because He first loved us. [20] Whoever claims to love God yet hates a brother or sister is a liar. For whoever does not love their brother and sister, whom

they have seen, cannot love God, whom they have not seen. [21]
And He has given us this command: Anyone who loves God must also love their brother and sister.

- 1 John 4:16-21

Mom was my resource for this book. Any question I had about family history, I went to her. She played a major role in this book series becoming a reality. Unless you are a judge who is reading this at the trial where she is suing me for co-author rights. If that's the case, she had nothing to do with the book. I don't even know who this woman is. Allegedly, she sent me the following text:

If God is leading you, you will write what he gives you; and it will not go out void. I had a woman once that told me God had told her that from me, those with depression would be helped and delivered. I remember thinking how could that be, I didn't know anything about depression. Since then, I have battled anxiety and limited worries and depression. But after the first time I heard you share your story, it wasn't directly by me, but from me that I felt this would be fulfilled. As I read the messages of all those kids[5], so many talked about struggles and anxiety and how your words and life had helped them. I didn't realize how many people, and so young, were so overwhelmed. You have made a difference in the lives of others, just as you always wanted. God may be opening a new door, with a new medium to help more.

I pray my mom is right. That is my mission in life: to stop others from enduring the struggles I did. Before that day in Peru when I shared my authentic "happy and crappy", my depression and bouts of anxiety had been the defining features of my life because I clung so tightly to hiding them. They impacted every single second of my life and everything I did or did not do. Once I embraced them, they became just one of my many characteristics. I decided then and have held firm to that resolve to this day, that shame would no longer force me to keep my

---

[5] *she's referring to my good-bye message I posted to my students once I retired from teaching and their comments back to me*

mental health issues hidden in the shadows. Some of my traits are good. Some are bad. But all of them are me. I am finally real. What the world sees is me, and I will continue to be that person. I will not waste another second living the life I think others want for me. Anxiety and depression will always be a part of me, but they are not me. I am more. I deserve what we all deserve: love. I am beautiful, important, and worthy. I am enough.

- Yes, I suffer from episodes of extreme, nearly debilitating anxiety as well as daily sensations of suffocation, heaviness in my chest, and feeling like I'm on the verge of gagging.
- No, that does not make me:
  - Weak
  - Broken
  - Ashamed
  - Alone
  - Unloved
  - Empty
  - Lacking
  - Unfaithful
- Yes, I have struggled with depression my entire adult life and, unless God heals me, I will battle it my whole life.
- Yes, I am also:
  - Strong
  - Intelligent
  - Honest
  - Dependable
  - Giving
  - A leader
  - A role-model
  - Devilishly handsome
    - Okay, maybe not that one. Still though, lots of good stuff there.

My greatest wish is that one day, a long time from now, Georgia will be at my bedside like I was for George as I'm breathing my last breath. I pray that on that day, I can give her the gift George gave me. Just like he did, I'll tell her if she wants to see me again, she'll have to stay close to God. I pray I have lived a life that lets her know this is true. I pray I have taught her there is an eternity to spend, and she can see her daddy again in Heaven. Through her life, she may veer so far from God's path, just as I did, that it seems she could never find her way back. When she doesn't feel worthy of love, she can think of her Daddy. She can think, "When did my Daddy love me more: when I was a good girl or a bad girl? Both. The same. All the time." Hopefully, my life for her can be what George and Dad's lives were for me: a light that leads the way back to God's path. Then, one day she'll be on her deathbed and tell her kids if they want to see her again, they have to stay close to God. From the life she's lived, they'll know it's true. The gift of God's love is eternal and will be passed from generation to generation.

I spent my whole life trying to be important so I could be what George and Dad deserved for me to be. I thought that was what mattered, but now I know better. Eventually, no one will remember my name or anything I've done on this Earth. That's okay because it's not about me. Many generations from now, my family will have love. Maybe they'll think that love started with Georgia's great grandson. When his kids say that his love changed their life, he'll tell them, "No, it wasn't me. I saw love first in my Dad/Mom." If he were to say the same to his Dad/Mom, they'd say, "No, no, it started with my mommy, Georgia." I know Georgia will be able to tell them, "Oh no, kids. When I questioned if there was love in the world and wanted to give up, the love of my Daddy kept me going."

Writing this today, I know the truth about the love in our family. I know if it hadn't been for George Alan West, that love would've ended with me. I know because I was there when I woke up in a jail cell with drug dealers, wife beaters, and a man vowing to murder his ex-wife. I was there when I was all alone, and I couldn't keep going. I was there when my shame and lies had finally been unearthed and the world knew how vile, weak, and pathetic I really was. I was there when I had to carry my daughter's car seat into school in shame because I couldn't drive. I was there all of those times when Georgia wasn't with me and I almost gave up on love. I was there all the times I wanted to give up, and I would think, "Would Bubby be proud of me?" In every situation, I would take that next step forward because he deserved for his life to be worth something. I didn't give up because I couldn't give up. I couldn't give up on him. I knew if I threw my life away, I was throwing away his as well. Of all the darkness I faced—the shame, the depression, the anxiety—his love for me and my love for him was greater. So, I kept going. I kept going when the only thing I had left to cling to was that love.

I struggled for a long time to explain why George meant so much to me. I finally opened up to my brother and talked about my struggles with George's death. He opened my eyes to the truth of everything that happened the day George died. George's life actually fulfilled what Mark 12:30-31 tells us are the greatest commandments. George loved God with his heart, his soul, his body, and his mind. He loved God with everything in him. And, from that place of love for God, he could love his neighbor as himself. Christ was the only perfect and righteous man to ever live. None of us will reach that goal, but we are to strive to be Christ-like. George got closer to this than anyone I ever knew. He was Christ-like. To remind myself of this, I have a tattoo on my rib cage that reads:

Having loved his own who were in the world, He loved them to the end. - John 13:1

My tattoo is on my side to signify where they pierced Jesus to make sure He was dead before they took Him off the cross. Christ didn't just tell us how to live, he was the example of how to do it. He loved us until the very end. Christ staked his love to the cross. I believe with all my heart that He looked out over time and saw me, you, and all of us. He saw me lying on the jail floor, exactly where I deserved to be with the other criminals. He saw me with a drug-addicted homeless man in there for publicly beating his girlfriend. He saw me there with the father and son who were selling heroin and the son claiming he would murder his ex-wife for turning him in when he got out. He saw me with the man who was going to jail for three years after his fourth DUI. He saw me there with them, where I deserved to be. And He loved me anyway. And He loved them. And you. He looked out over time and saw us all at our lowest points, and He loved us. He knew I would never be able to get up off of that floor without Him. Physically, sure, I would've walked out of the jail still. But mentally, emotionally, and as a man, my life would've ended there. The shame and guilt were just too much for me to bear. He knew without Him sacrificing His life for me, I could never make it.

Wherever you are in life, He loves you the same. He sees you too. The nails did not hold Him to the cross. I did. And you did. We have never had to wonder if He truly loves us since. God loved us enough to give His only Son, the King of all kings, for us. I believe the most natural thing in the world when you really accept that somebody loves is to try to return that love. The way for us to show we love God with our heart, soul, mind, and strength is to love our neighbor as ourselves.

He loved me until the very end. And so did George. He loved me until his very last breath. I kept going when everything in my life had crumbled away because my love for George remained. Today, I am over two years sober. Eventually my love for George pointed me to an ever greater love, my love for Christ and His love for me. George's life gave me the chance to get back up and keep going when I couldn't do it on my own. He gave me the chance to be a man that Georgia would be proud to call Daddy. He gave me the tears I'm crying right now, tears that are finally of joy instead of shame. He gave me the determination to always push forward. Georgia deserves that from me too. I know the truth. Love is real.

My life, Georgia's life, and my family on down the line until we are no more, we are all different because of George. For my family, it started with George. I wanted to live a life that would make everyone know George's name. I thought that would make all of his pain worth it. If people just knew him and what he went through. Even so, as the years roll by and the generations pile up, the memories of George will fade. Eventually, no one will know his name, but his love will remain. It won't do so automatically though. Each person has to take up that mantle and dedicate their life to love. With every breath I have to give, I will love. I am living proof that people can change. I love George as much today as the day he died. It will never fade. One day I'll be gone and Georgia will have to carry on without me. But our love will never end. Whatever she faces in her life, she will always have her Daddy's love to fall back on. If she accepts my love for her is real even in those darkest of times, then love itself must be real. And, where love exists, there is always hope. Love isn't a story with a happy ending. Love is a story with no ending.

Love Life Challenge

Notice the difference in this challenge. It's not for a single action. It is for life.

In the opening lesson, I talked about my failure and the lowest moment of my life. It was the first night I realized I would not be with Georgia every day. There will be times in her life that she will cry for her Daddy, and I won't be there. It was the night I realized I had let her down. I had lost everything in the world that had ever mattered to me. I have had so much failure in my life, and my refusal to forgive myself perpetuated my struggles. Some of you will be able to relate to the specifics of my story, but some of you won't. Maybe you've struggled with the loss of a loved one too, or perhaps you are the victim of abuse. There's a chance you have battled addiction as well, or maybe you have done something morally wrong that you feel is unforgivable. I don't know the specifics of your story, but I do know this: we have all fallen. We have all felt loss and struggled. We have all been less than we are. Although our wounds are all different, the spark to start the healing process is universal: acceptance. You have to accept that the pain is real. You have to open the door to experience the hurt. It may be brutal. It will definitely be difficult. But it is necessary. When you open that door to feel the pain, you also open it to feel joy. You allow peace, love, and all that is good in the world to enter as well.

I was allowed to keep my teaching certificate and continued in the profession for another year. At the end of that year, I chose to walk away from teaching because I felt God was leading me on a different path. Still, that ultimately doesn't matter. I learned that everything can be taken. They could've taken my ability to teach. I could've lost my home, my truck, and everything I own. It is all temporary. If someone wanted, they could even take my life. But they cannot take my love. I'll carry it with me until the end. George has been gone sixteen years. If he had given me a million dollars, it would all be gone by now. But he didn't. He gave me love. And I love him as much today as I ever did. It has not faded because our love is eternal.

He gave me the greatest gift I could've ever received; He pointed me in the direction of Christ. He lived a life that let me know Christ was real. No one can take Christ's love from me or you. From the second He died on that cross, you were His, and He was yours. Once I peeled away all of the superficial layers of pride I had covered my life with, Christ's love for me still remained. Once I finally, truly accepted Christ's love for me, I accepted His forgiveness. In that, I also accepted that I had to forgive myself. Trying to carry my sin and burden alone as an act penance is to deny the sacrifice He made on the cross. We had a lesson about forgiveness, and that same message applies to forgiving yourself. As long as you withhold forgiveness from yourself, you will forever be a slave to whatever you have done. He hung there for you. He took your place. When does He love us more? When we are good or when we are bad? Both. The same. All the time.

We cling to so much that we believe is important but that will eventually be gone. What is at the very center of your life? What defines you? If the most important thing in your world isn't that you are a child of Christ, then I invite you to change your life now. I beg you to avoid all the pain and struggle I went through. Become truly strong by admitting that you are truly weak. Yield to the Almighty that allowed you to be here in the first place. Give up all those things we think matter that do not: esteem, approval, pleasure, safety, security. And in that place come to rely on God. Do that today, and tomorrow, and the next today, and for eternity. God is love, and love is real.

A personal invitation

I provide Christians with a holistic wellness plan to love
themselves and accept they are enough.

Please visit **www.loveisrealwellness.com** to schedule a FREE
30-minute *Live Better Consultation* session with me. Join my
Live Better, Love More Program to begin a new life today.

Contact me at loveisrealwellness@gmail.com

Learn about all the ways we're trying to make the world a better
place at:
- Facebook, Instagram, YouTube - @LoveIsRealWellness
  - For behind the scenes information about each
    lesson of the book, check out my *"A Real
    Minute"* videos starting at Episode 32 where I
    will go *"Beyond the Book."*
- Twitter - @LoveIsRealWell1 (the last character is a
  one...Twitter had to be difficult with the name
  limitations)

My problems were anxiety, depression, and shame. Those may
not be your issues. But we all certainly have problems. Those
problems all boil down to the same basic questions.
Am I enough?
Do I have what it takes?
The way you think, sleep, eat, and exercise are medicine.
Literally. I founded *Love is Real Wellness* so I could fulfill
God's purpose: to love you, to help you love yourself, and for us
both to go love the world.
The habits in my *Live Better, Love More Program* all have
complex science beneath each. The program will have actual
biological effects on your body in the same way that prescribed
medications do. If you could harness these powers and put them

in a pill, you'd be a billionaire. But the power isn't in a pill. It's in you.

My 20-week *Live Better, Love More Program* starts with Part 1 (*Live Better*). The first 10-weeks, you will bring holistic wellness to your life through science-backed habits that will change your body by changing how you: 1) Think, 2) Sleep, 3) Live, 4) Eat, 5) Exercise. Part 2 (*Love More*) covers the last 10-weeks where everything is completely personalized to your needs to address any of the following issues:

Anger	Focus	Perfectionism
Anxiety	Gut Issues	Shame/Regrets
Athletic Performance	Happiness	Sleep
Brain Health	Headaches	Slowing Anger
Closer Relationships	High Blood Pressure	Stress
Creativity	Kindness to Yourself	Type 2 Diabetes
Depression	Leadership	Weight Loss
Energy	Overthinking	Wellbeing
Family Health	Pain	

Optimize Mental Functionality	Perform Better Physically	Reduce Health Problems	Slow Aging	Strengthen Relationships	Defeat Shame
Enhance Focus and Concentration	Increase Lean Muscle Mass	Reduce Inflammation and Resulting -Type 2	Increase Energy	Find Forgiveness For Others	Lessen Anxiety
Heighten sense of calm	Lose Weight	-Alzheimer's -Heart	Reduce Pain -Neck	Improve Quality of	Lessen Depression
Improve attention	Improve Body Composition	-Heart Attack -Arthritis	-Shoulders -Back	Increase Quantity of	Enhance Sense of Well-being
Improve cognitive	Increse Strength	-Stroke	-Hips -Knees	Increase Libido	Improve Mood
Improve decision	Improved Clarity	Lower Blood Pressure	Improve Sleep		Find Forgiveness
Improve memory	Improved Focus	Improve Cardiac Health	Boost Immune System		Reduce Stress

Testimonials

Because of Adam, I have the inspiration to take a chance and make a career doing something I know will not only make me happy but will help others as well. I truly believe I would not have found my calling without his help.
-Linda C. Richmond, KY

The questions Adam asked me were insightful and made me understand myself better. I've been finding myself overwhelmed with all of the moving pieces to a life-changing decision I have to make. Having an unbiased mediator really helped me to understand everything I have to consider and how to ultimately get to where I want to be.
    -Emma M. Miami, FL

Letter to Georgia

This is the only part of this entire series not edited by my talented friend Jake Bingham. He turned my incoherent ramblings into legible English. This letter was written on my phone before I began my book-writing endeavor while I struggled with the decision to do this or not. When I decided to move forward with the concept, I wrote this letter to Georgia before beginning. I knew it would be tough to relive my struggles and to open up all of my personal wounds for the world to see. Still, I was okay with that. Nonetheless, I didn't want to let Georgia down. It was a struggle to let her know the truth of who I once was. This was my letter to her.

My angel,

I am so sorry, baby. I am so sorry for the things I've done. I am so sorry that you have to know. You're too young to understand all of this right now. I want you to be proud of me. I am sorry for all the times you haven't been. When we pray at night, I always end by asking God to help me be a better Daddy for you. I hope you remember that when you're old. You always tell me that I don't need to pray for that because I'm already the best Daddy in the world. The things in this book are why I have to pray every night for strength to be better. Alone, I am weak. I have let you and the people I love down again and again. Hopefully, you can read this 50 years from now and I'll be 52 years sober. I pray I've lived out those 50 years in a way you can be proud of.

I hope you can feel the same way about me as I do my dad, but I'm writing to you so you don't make the same mistake I did. Don't think that you have to take on the world by yourself. I want you to know that I am not the answer. I have never been the answer. The answer is Christ. He turned me from what I was to what I am today. If somewhere along life's road I turn my back on Christ, you'll know this is true. I'll turn back to drinking. I'll turn back to who I was. I'll have a life of misery and shame that I desperately try to cover in good deeds.

I want you to grow up to be successful. I want you to grow up to find a partner you love. I want you to have everything you deserve. Even so, if it comes to a choice to you finding those things and you finding Christ, I choose Christ every time. Live in a cardboard box under a bridge if that's what it takes. I hope you realize how much you lose when you lose Him. Your perspective on your life and all of life gets distorted when you don't make space for him, obscuring His love for you. Search for Him every day of your life. If you do that, you'll be a success. If you don't, you won't. Be a success, my angel.

You were the only thing that mattered more than my pride. God put you in my life to give me a chance. Hold on to that love. If you ever get to a point where everything seems to be upside down and there doesn't seem to be hope, remember how much I love you. If you accept that my love for you is real, then love itself has to be real. Love is more real than anything in this world and is greater than anything you will ever face. If you read this again once I'm gone, stay close to God, and I'll see you again someday. We'll be able to share our love forever. Give that love to the world. Make it a better place.

Never forget - When does daddy love you more? When you are a good girl or a bad girl? Both. All the time. Forever.

Love,

Your Daddy

George In Their Own Words

☐ Pat Reid, my mom

    ☐ I don't know if I can truly put into words all that George meant to me. I was 10 years older than him, and both Dave and George always felt like they were my own babies instead of my little brothers. Our family revolved around George, and we all cherished and loved him. I think that by his example, and the grace with which he faced his challenges, he helped shape not only the lives of our family, but all those who came to know him. Just by the life he lived, he taught us to appreciate the little things, to show appreciation to others, and to never take a day for granted. I believe without a doubt, I would not be the person I am today without him as part of my life. His faith and strength strongly influenced my own life and relationship with God. So many people have shared stories of how special he was to them through the years. One of the nurses from Saint Joseph of Lexington contacted me on social media a few years ago, to tell me how George had impacted the doctors and nurses who had worked with him. She shared that the doctor who had completed his triple transplant and overseen his care for the 10 years following had cried at his bedside after his death. She said this was the first time she had seen this happen. A grief counselor who worked at the hospital when he passed away contacted Mom and Dad not long after his death. She said she had never seen anyone die with the grace and manner that he did, and he was only 29 years old. As he knew he was living his last moments of life, he took the time to thank the doctors and nurses who had cared for him, to send messages of love and appreciation to his loved ones. He encouraged my sons to get saved, and to remember him by watching Star Wars for him. He lifted his hands in praise to his Lord. George was special; he is special. He lives on in my memories. I see him in my sons, who both have so many characteristics like him. We were so blessed for God to have placed George Alan West in our lives: My love, my baby, my friend. Oh how I long to hear him laugh and say, "I love you, Sissy" just one more time. Soon I will meet him again, and then we will not be parted again.

☐ Tyler Wolfe, George's friend

☐ George West, to me, was one of the strongest male role-models I remember having as a teenager. Of course I couldn't know to what extent, but I knew George lived every day with pain. With that being said, he never let that stop him from smiling every day and keeping a positive attitude. I always thought he seemed like he was living every day as if it would be the last time he would see the people he was around in the way he spoke to and treated people. It was always with kindness, empathy, and more than anything, respect. That is what I admired most about George and what is, more than anything, a trait of his I have tried to carry on in my own life and hopefully pass along to my children in seeing that in me. When you spoke with George you really knew that he wasn't just nodding his head at key parts of your story. He was truly listening to and caring about what you had to say. A quick example of that to leave you with: One day George, Alan, Dirty Darrell, and myself were at Soundtrax in Corbin. The wall was covered from floor to ceiling in various posters. I spotted a Texas Chainsaw Massacre poster, and that being my favorite movie, I commented on how much I liked it. I, myself, never thought more about that comment. A couple weeks or so later it was my birthday. My mom came to my room to let me know that George was outside. I go to the door and see he has a rolled up poster in his hand. I can still hear him say "happy birthday, Smilly" as he handed it to me. I unrolled it to find that exact Texas Chainsaw Massacre poster. Not one like it but that same one from Soundtrax complete with pinholes from where it had been hanging on their wall. All these years later I think about that both every time I see the movie or every year on my birthday. Someone I thought was so cool and admired and had so much respect for noticed such a small comment I made and cared enough to go out of his way to make that happen for me. I hope George knew and I want his family to know what an impact he had on me and that I hope to let those great qualities of George live on through me and my children so that they may never be forgotten, even by those who never had the amazing opportunity to meet him.

☐ Dave West, George's brother

☐ There are very few people that I'm around for very long that I don't tell them about my brother George. Something that is special to me and that I think of often was a conversation me and George were having about the Bible, and he told me his favorite Bible verse was Matthew 17:20. He lived by this, and if you don't know what it says, then look it up. That's what he told me to do when he told me it was his favorite verse and I asked what it said. I remember the exact date that he told me this. His birthday is next week and he would have been 46. He has been gone 16 years and it seems like yesterday.

☐ Richard Sester, George's friend and the artist for the covers for the entire *Love is Real* Series

☐ I first met George when I was a sophomore in high school. We had art class together and quickly became friends. We bonded over drawing, music, and, of course, Star Wars. George was extremely talented and funny. He had tons of friends. That was evident on the weekends when his car would be packed full of people riding around with him and socializing. Some of my favorite memories from the mid to late 90's include George. There were many trips to the movies, trips to Recordsmith in Richmond or SoundTrax in Corbin to get new music, concerts, and many hours of just riding around and hanging out. George will always be one of my best friends and the time we shared will always be looked back on fondly and with a smile. I miss him greatly and think of him often.

☐ Randy Rader, George's friend

☐ I had the pleasure to meet George and become friends with him in high school. We both had the same interests in music, but music aside, he was a great friend. The biggest thing I remember of George was his smile and laugh, his happy genuine personality. Everytime I'd see him out it seemed like we'd carry on a conversation for a while, but the last conversation I can remember like it was yesterday. His health was failing again and he needed another procedure. He told me he was tired and didn't think he could do it again. I held it together for the rest of our chat and we parted ways with a goodbye and a smile. Made me realize life is so short and to never take life for granted.

☐ Heather Crawford Rutledge, George's friend

☐ George was a friend to me like no other. He listened to me and soothed my fragile teenage soul with his wisdom and his heart. He saw the good in everyone, but was very quick to defend his friends if need be. I struggle to find words to explain how much he meant to me because a linguist would have to invent a new language to create a word meaningful enough for George. The hours we spent riding around in his car, listening to music, laughing, and just being friends, I remember those days as being some of the best times of my life. When I moved to Richmond for college, he was a constant fixture in our apartment and his presence was more appreciated than he ever could have realized. I lie awake in bed at night sometimes thinking about him, and how I regret not letting him know how much he meant to me while he was still on this earth. I will never know another like him. I loved him and I miss him.

☐ Tabitha Smith, George's friend

☐ George came into my life as a mysterious figure on mIRC known only as Turd Burglar, real identity unknown to pretty much everyone. We always had the best chats and most interesting conversations and I looked forward to him logging on daily. It was the highlight of my day. I don't remember when he revealed his real identity to me but our friendship only grew from that point. I remember spending many evenings with him at the softball field just hanging out watching the good ol' bus garage team. He was smart, kind, and funny. He introduced me to new music that I would have never given a second thought to at the time as well as films. His love of Star Wars was endless and his collection was out of this world. I think of George often and sitting in the halls of Saint Joseph Main as some of his final days were upon him. This world got a little dimmer when George left it. I am thankful to say he was a part of my life and will forever be in my memories.

☐ Angela Gray Rice, George's friend

☐ I remember he could draw anything. He enjoyed life—there was hardly a time you could be around him that you were not laughing at his jokes and stories.

- Lisa Mays, my Dad's sister
  - George was and will always be very special to so many. Even though he was very sick, I never did hear him complain about it. He was very talented in so many different ways. His drawings, creativity, and imagination were beyond words. Love and miss him.
- Chris Shawn Fields, George's friend
  - George was a giant! He was wise way beyond his years and he was chill like no other person I have ever met! Loved being in art class with him and in life! I'm getting close to the end of one of my careers and embarking on my pastoral call, and I'm reflecting back on things I've been through and people who have greatly affected me. I can say, of all the people that have, George is at the top! George has more Heart than anyone I have ever known, and I truly mean I loved that dude! He was a legend in my book!
- D Irvin Thompson, George's friend
  - Loved George. When he was in the hospital the last time a day before his death, he told his family to make sure they returned a movie he had rented from my store. All the things he should have been doing the last few days of his life, he thought about a simple movie rental. No words can describe George? Well, "Beautiful."
- Leigh Anne Fields Smith, George's friend
  - George to me was always the life of the party. He kept everyone around him cracking up, including me. I will never forget at a get-together we both attended someone there was pretending to tell your fortune. It must have been around Halloween but anyway, he was the most serious that I had ever seen George. It was also right before his transplant surgery. He said to the fortune teller "Am I going to live through this

surgery and be normal again?" It about broke me down that night because I had never seen such seriousness in him. It also showed me how short and precious life really is! George was one of a kind and I will never forget him.

- Janine Morgan, George's cousin and friend
  - I miss George so much! As far as memories go, the ones that stick out to me most...George wanted a tattoo so bad; I took him and he got the scorpion on his leg. We tried to keep it hush hush. We knew Momma and Aunt Lou was going to be mad. Secret didn't last long. I also won't ever forget George wrecking you (Adam), me, and Alan getting off the parkway!
  - Oh and George's ninja stuff and four wheeler when we were little; I thought was the coolest stuff I'd ever seen! I got all my hair cut off and spiked like a boy and started wearing camo while riding my four wheeler because I wanted to be like him.
  - Here's another. I had just got tanning beds put in at one of the convenience stores. I got George to draw a big poster to hang on the wall above the tanning bed doors for advertisement. He drew a sexy woman that was pretty much naked! I still put it up and dad made me take it down!
- Lorean Hicks, George's grade school teacher
  - George was in my class and he would fuss with his mommy to stay a little longer with his friends. I will always remember him wanting me to leave the room so he could be storyteller. He would include all the children in his stories. I would go to the office and flip down the intercom button to listen mostly to make sure all was okay. He was truly loved and had a vivid imagination.
- Jocelyn Wolfe, George's high school biology teacher
  - George was a student in my Advanced Biology class when he was a freshman at CCHS. He was

such a determined young man. If I remember correctly, he would come to school each day and stay as long as he could before becoming so weak that he would have to go home and rest. He was so intelligent and talented. His biological drawings were the most beautiful that I'd ever seen. I used examples of his work for several years to inspire other students to do their best. I will never forget George's high school graduation. He was so handsome in his cap and gown. Sad to say that by the time everyone was lined up and ready to walk in the procession, he became weak and could not stay to walk across the stage. I re-told George's life many times over the years to inspire other students to make the most use of their talents. I would tell them of a young man who strived beyond his limits every day of his life. George was an inspiration to everyone who knew him.

☐ Betty Bailey, George's cousin
☐ I always remember how you and your brother always loved and looked up to George. He was and will always be a Hero to you both. Your mom was a second mom to him. Alison always loved him so much, and him, Alison, Tammy, and Sonya always enjoyed being together. You can bet there was always some good, fun, mischief brewing.

☐ Brandon Howard, my childhood friend
☐ I'll always remember him being at the ballfields every summer and around the football field in the fall. One of the kindest and caring souls you'd ever get a chance to meet. Always found the best in others.

☐ Wesley Whitehead, George's friend
☐ George was awesome. Inspired my hair color choices for years to come.

☐ Chris Cavanaugh, George's childhood friend

- I remember goofing off with him in art class all the time. We had many laughs in class.
- Travis Marcum, George's friend
  - I think of what a kind person he was. I also can't think of George without thinking of Deftones and White Zombie.
- Ken Bolin, pastor of Manchester Baptist Church
  - George was a thoughtful, courageous young man who fought every day to live. He made the best of each new day. He was my hero!
- Ralph Strong, coach of Big Creek Grade School football team where George served as the manager
  - George was an inspiration to everyone around him! He was such a big part of the good old days of Big Creek football!
- Lillian Baker, George's cousin
  - Love that smile. I'm sure that was an awesome trip for him. As sick as he was, he still smiled and laughed a lot.
- Ruth Estep, George's friend
  - He was the nicest, sweetest person ever.

Bible verses used in *Love is Real*

Genesis 2:5-6	Matthew 18:3	2 Corinthians 11:23-33
Exodus 4:10	Mark 10:27	2 Corinthians 12:7-10
Numbers 12:3	Mark 10:43-45	Galatians 6:7
Numbers 20:2-12	Luke 9:23	Ephesians 4:32
Joshua 1:9	Luke 18:27	Ephesians 6:19-20
Joshua 24:15 (partial)	Luke 23:34	2 Timothy 3:16
1 Chronicles 28:9 (partial)	John 10:10	Hebrews 8:12
Psalms 37:23-24	John 17:24	Hebrews 11:1
Psalms 46:1-3	Acts 20:35	Hebrews 11:13
Psalms 103:9-13	Romans 5:8	Hebrews 11:16
Psalms 139:14	Romans 6:14	James 1:12
Psalms 147:3	Romans 6:21	James 4:13-15
Proverbs 17:22	Romans 7:18-19	1 Peter 4:10-11
Proverbs 20:5	Romans 8:28	2 Peter 1:5-9
Ecclesiastes 1:7-8	Romans 8:31-39	1 John 2:16-17
Jeremiah 29:11	Romans 12:2	1 John 4:16-21
Ezekiel 18:20	Romans 15:13	1 John 4:7-8
Matthew 6:1	1 Corinthians 15:31	1 John 4:12
Matthew 17:20	2 Corinthians 4:8-9	

Acknowledgements

Thank you so much for everyone who turned my dream into a reality. There has been so much work put into this book by so many people; I could never mention them all. I thank you all so, so much. Know that if I've forgotten and failed to mention you by name below, I am forever appreciative of your help.

- Jake Bingham - Editor
- Alan Reid - Cover page design, Love is Real Wellness logo design, Creative Director and Video Production for Love is Real Wellness
- Richard Sester - Cover page artwork
- Geddy Walker - Business Manager for Love is Real Wellness, LLC
- Zach Rankin - Website Designer and Social Media Director for Love is Real Wellness
- Hunter West, Luke Jones, and Susan Rahimzadeh - Junior Editors
- Beta Readers - I don't want to list everyone here because I'm afraid I will leave someone out. Please know how grateful I am for your contribution and how important you were to creating this book.
  - Pat Reid in particular provided me with lots of the history I needed for the book. And she read it about five times before it was ever released so she gets a specific shout out.

Sources

Life Application Bible Study Guide
Uncommon by Tony Dungy
Quiet strength by Tony Dungy
Emotionally Healthy Spirituality by Peter Scazzero
A Purpose Driven Life by Rick Warren
Your God is Too Small by J.B. Phillips
The Daily Office by Peter Scazzero
Not a Fan by Kyle Idleman
Make Disease Disappear by Dr. Rangan Chaterjee
The Depression Cure by Dr. Stephen Ilardi
Delighting in the Trinity by Michael Reeves
Kill the Spider by Carlos Whittaker
Loving God by Charles Colson
Grit by Angela Duckworth
Strong Father, Strong Daughter by Meg Meeker
The Mission Journal by David Iskander
Helping Without Hurting by Brian Fikkert and Steve Corbett
Life Is A Joke by The Javna Brothers
Jonathan James and the Whatif Monster by Michelle Nelson-Schmidt

Made in the USA
Monee, IL
02 January 2021

56104844R00125